Telementation

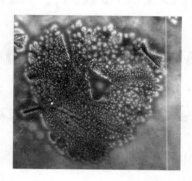

Cosmic Feeling
and the Law of
Attraction

by Jeffrey Grupp

Telementation

Cosmic Feeling and the

Law of Attraction

© *Jeffrey Grupp*

Published by ProgressivePress.com, PO Box 126,
Joshua Tree, Calif., 92252

Third edition, published January, 2011.

Printed in Malaysia

Length: 120 pages; 22,000 words

ISBN-10: 1-61577-552-8   EAN 978-1-61577-552-1

LCCN: 2010292069

BISAC Classification codes:

OCC010000   BODY, MIND & SPIRIT / Meditation
PHI025000   PHILOSOPHY / Zen
PSY003000   PSYCHOLOGY / Applied Psychology

2011

Contents

For Amy, Amelia, and Chloe.

And for the citizens of the world everywhere, who, whether they know it or not, are trying to awaken from the dark night of the soul and from the nightmare of history.

The basic premise is that energy follows thought. Wherever you place you attention, energy follows.

—Richard Gordon, *Quantum Touch*

In the lightening flash is truth.

—*Kausītaki Upanisad* IV.2

In short, everything appears to be wrong in me because the fundamental idea that everything is perfectly, eternally and totally positive, is asleep in the centre of my being, because it is not awakened, living and active therein.

—Hubert Benoit, *Zen and the Psychology of Transformation*

Therefore I say unto you, What things soever ye desire, when ye pray, believe that ye receive them, and ye shall have them.

—Jesus, Mark 11:24 (King James Version)

You can learn to create what you want using energy and thought rather than physical effort, and produce results that go beyond anything you can create with physical effort alone.

—Sanaya Roman and Duane Packer, *Creating Money*

"He insulted me, he hurt me, he defeated me, he robbed me." Those who think such thoughts will not be free from hate... For hate is not conquered by hate: hate is conquered by love. This is a law eternal. Many do not know that we are here in this world to live in harmony. Those who know this do not fight against each other.

—Buddha (*Dhammapada* v. 3, 5, and 6.)

Jesus answered them,
"Is it not written in your law, I said, Ye are gods?"

—Jesus, John 10:34 (King James Version)

What is the purpose of life? It is joy.
What is the reason of life? It is joy.
What is the basis of life? It is freedom.
What is the result of life? It is expansion.
What is the reason you came forth in this physical experience? You wanted more.
You wanted more exposure to more opportunity to have more feelings.
So, ... the meaning of life is *life*.
It's to feel life pouring through you.

. —Esther and Jerry Hicks

Opening poem...

I feel,

> *Inside me,*
>
> *Inside you,*

Causing leafy plants to grow up around us,

Air turns into flowers,

Like radiating stars,

Intoxicating the world,

Expanding our pineal glands,

Our eyes are prompted to close,

The world is covered,

By the ultra-radiant white light,

That is emanating from our hearts.

Definitions

Consciousness: the ineffable, holy "entity" through which you have experiences (feelings, meanings, thoughts, visualizations, holy experiences). Consciousnesses are not distinguishable from one another (my feeling of love in my consciousness feels just like yours does to you and thus they are indistinguishable, as all conscious contents are), they are interdimensional, and not distinguishable from the energy that composes all of reality, and thus focusing of consciousness is a focusing (amplification) of energy. Consciousness is the creative power of reality.

Religion: there are many definitions of this word, but in this book I equate the word "religion" with the words "spirituality", "transcendental", "religious experience", "ecstasy", "meditation", and "spirit". I do not mean "religion" to have something to do with war or genocide, but rather with elevated consciousness via meditation.

Religious experience: the process of altering your consciousness in some ways that change your mental states toward increased feelings of happiness and knowledge, to the degree that you feel you are taking part in something greater than your ordinary egotistical life (your body and your immediate survival-level concerns), and taking part in the ineffable holiness of the universe.

Telementation: the perpetual process of reality being created by the deep inner states of consciousness that endlessly stream through sentient life-forms.

You Must Feel Your Innate, Ineffable, Ever-present Joy Within You, or You Will Not Succeed at Telementation ("The Law of Attraction")

The power within you which enables you to form a thought-picture is the starting point of all there is.

—Genevieve Behrend[1]

This book is about Telementation, which is a specific kind of meditation that centers on the "law of attraction." In summary, what this book shows you is that if you *know* and *feel* something deeply enough within your consciousness, it will materialize in physical reality. In other words, if a person *knows* and *feels* that, for example, his wife will have a particularly good day, and he knows it without a shadow of doubt, so convinced that this is true that he feels it at the deepest parts of his being, it will occur without exception in physical reality. *Telementation is the principal law of the cosmos*: the way you feel about reality at your innermost being will become how reality is structured. For example, if you feel, at your innermost being, that reality is joyous and prosperous for humans, then your life and those around you will have joy and prosperity. This is the most powerful force in the universe, all of us have it and can utilize it *right now*, and it is our absolute key to personal safety and protection, deep inner satisfaction and happiness, and to profound social justice worldwide.

Why such a short book on mastering the law of attraction? Because one does not master the law of attraction by reading 200, 300, or 400 page books. One learns to master the Law of Attraction by *practicing* it! There are some key points you need to know before you practice and while you are learning how to steer and control the law of attraction, but those can be easily expounded in a few dozen pages, and after that, you will master it, and thus have anything you want, only if you *practice*.

Here is one of the most important things you will read in this book:

You have to find joy in your Law of
Attraction exercises and practice—what I
will call "telementation" hereafter—if you
are going to succeed: if it's not fun, you

won't stick with it and you won't have

success no matter how determined you are.

How do you do this? Your telementation meditation must be *religious ecstasy*, at least to some degree—sort of like what St. Teresa, Buddha, or the Hindu ecstatics have expressed. You don't have to be falling down, blinded by the light of God everyday, like St. Paul on the Road to Damascus; but you will need to learn to transform your life, to at least some degree, into a life of spiritual/religious happiness. This is what you will learn in this book, and trust me, it's easy, and it's what you've been longing for deep down, all of your life!

In actuality, religious ecstasy is what telementation really is, at its core, and thus when you practice it properly, you will want to practice it more and more, since it is a form of religious happiness. This is a happiness likely far deeper than any happiness you have ever felt hitherto, far deeper than what television, culture, chasing money, church, or chit-chat can ever give you. It is something akin to the profound soul-level joy you felt when you looked into your child's eyes for the first time, the day they were born. True telementation is easy to learn, and is the bliss of Thoreau in his forest home, the peace of Gandhi saving the citizens of India, and it is the lightening-joy of a flower softly opening as birds sing in the morning.

The core of the meditation of telementation is ineffable joy and freedom, because the core of *you* is ineffable joy and freedom. If you have not discovered this, then that is just because you have not taken the time to look within yourself to see what you are made of, which is joy, divinity, light, and freedom. Why do you think it says in Genesis 1 that you are created in God's image? That means that you (you = your deepest inner consciousness) are ineffable joy and freedom since you are "in God's image" in your innermost self.

In order to succeed with the law of attraction (telementation), you need to gradually make telementation meditation a central focus in your life—not obsessively, but joyfully. Other books on the law of attraction that tell you that you need to just sit for five minutes or so each day practicing it are not correct, for reasons I will explain later in this book. Those who follow those books will likely fail (and I have listened to seemingly countless students of mine who have told me all about their failures when, following such books, they first started working with me on the "law of attraction"). Therefore, we need to be able to carry out telementation meditation easily, happily, and in times of stress too, when you have spare moments when you are, for example, walking the dog, getting the mail, brushing your teeth, driving or biking to work, laying in bed as you fall asleep at night (one of my personal favorites), and so on.

For these reasons, if you are not religiously joyful in your practice, filled with at least some sort of spiritual happiness, *and thus wanting to do the practice of telementation as much as anything you do at any part of any given day,* working from your God-illuminated, energy-intensive core of your self, feeling that God-drunken happiness, *there is no way you will succeed.* You must first develop (uncover) your inner Godhood, and then start the simple exercises of telementation meditation. You must be looking forward to your telementational practice more than anything in the world, and then you will succeed, and you will feel what you have never felt before, and you will feel what you have always longed for: the infinite light of divinity that is everywhere.

Life is immensely busy for most of us, and we will fail at the law of attraction unless we can do it in the spare moments of our lives when we have little pockets of time. And practicing it is, you will see, deeply peaceful, soulful, enjoyable, and spiritual. In fact, you will see when you learn the practice, the art, of the meditation of the telementation, that the deep feelings you have when you are in the mode of telementation meditation *is what you really are*: what you've always longed to feel, the peace you've always longed for, and it is the satisfaction that you've always had at your core even though you did not know it. *You will never be happier than when you are in a telementational mode of consciousness.* It is a peace you cannot fathom from your ordinary, egotistical state of consciousness.

So telementation is not *just* about getting what you want (more appropriately put, getting what you *will* yourself to receive), it's also about feeling as good as you've ever felt, literally all the time, and literally injecting that radiance into all people and life-forms around you. What a world we would live in if our schools taught the information in this book from the time that children were young!

Why *This* Book?

Human origins lie in the stars.

—Paul Von Ward, *Gods, Genes, and*
Consciousness

So, why *another* book about telementation (the law of attraction), you might ask, when there are already several books on the subject that others have written? Answer: because this book has two things that the others apparently have not included: (1) information on carrying-out telementation through feeling and thought, rather than primarily through thought, and (2) detailed instructions on how telementation is meditation, and what specifically you are to do in telementation meditation, as we learn how to carry out the law of attraction. To my knowledge, other books do not involve these, but they are essential in learning and carrying out telementation, and this must be the reason so many fail when trying to learn telementation/ law of attraction. They are, without question, the keys to success. I am, frankly, confused as to why the other books on this subject have so readily overlooked these critical issues. But I suspect that their doing so is one of the key reasons why literally every single student I have had who has come to me saying they have been attempting to learn the law of attraction through other books has found nothing but frustration and failure. I do not mean to attack these other books; I actually like some of them quite a bit, and I have learned a lot through some of them. I am merely asserting that I think they are too quickly passing over the key instructions that students need for success in telemementation; and more importantly, they are overlooking the key ingredient of telemementation/the law of attraction that everyone should be focused on more than any other issue during their telemementation practice: *feeling reality into existence, rather than just thinking it into existence.*

As stated above, when most people (well, *all*, in fact) who have first approached me to discuss their attempts in learning the law of attraction, I find that if they have read up on the subject from other sources, what they are doing is focusing their *thoughts*—focusing their thoughts in a specific way in order to attempt to will reality into existence in accord with their thoughts. And not a single person has come to me and told me that they have been successful in any way. That's pretty interesting: a 100 percent failure rate, according to my survey. But it's what I would most definitely expect, *because you can't carry out telemementation/the law of attraction that way. You have to do it by focusing your feelings firstly, and then secondly your thoughts,* and only via some rather specific feeling- and thought-modes as well, and which this book is devoted to exploring.

At their base, your feelings—those things inside you, that have always been inside you—are profoundly religious, containing religious ecstasy. It does not matter if you are thin or not, old or young, quick thinking or not, if you have feelings in you, then they, at their deep base, are religious-cosmic powers. Most likely you just have not noticed this, or have not known *how* to notice. From this inner religiosity and spiritualism that you all have deep within you, the cosmos is created. And from that inner soulfulness, telementation can be exercised. The point of this book is to specifically show how this is done.

If you forget or lose sight of the importance of the italicized words two paragraphs above, you will fail at the law of attraction, along with apparently millions of others who are failing. *Telementation is feeling+thought.* It is not just thought. Your consciousness creates reality, as the originators of the world's religions have told us for thousands of years. But your consciousness is not just thought, so why would we assume that telementation is carried out only through thought? It cannot, and it can only be carried out when all of consciousness (feeling+thought) is amplified, empowered, focused, and spiritualized. That's what I call telementation: *feeling* reality into existence as your will determines.[2]

This feeling-method of the law of attraction is not only easier than the thought-based method, it's *always* successful (you will see why below), once you learn to feel things a specific way that I will describe. The thought-based method is always unsuccessful.

Telementation

(aka, "The Law of Attraction")

If you are not happy *now*, then what are you
doing on this planet anyway?[3]

—Len Horowitz

Telementation is the greatest human power there is;
but very few humans know that it even exists.
Telementation is the theory that your deepest inner
consciousness creates reality, and all humans are, together,
creating reality and the world we live in via our innermost
consciousnesses.

For example, if I *believe and feel* deeply within
myself, in the most inner parts of my consciousness, that
reality is safe and wonderful, then my life will be safe and
wonderful for me. Or, as another example, if I believe that
reality is unsafe and dangerous, then danger and lack of
safety will come my way repeatedly.

But telementation is, actually, more specific than
that simple explanation: it is more dramatic and
metaphysical: if I believe and feel from my innermost
being that I am an ideal husband and father, then things
fall into place such that I act so that my wife and children

love me surprisingly deeply. Or, more startlingly, if I am playing basketball, and if I believe in a deep, specific way that the shot I am about to take, or am taking, will miss, then it will, indeed, *miss*—or if I believe and feel it will not miss, then it won't.

All of us have this incredible inner power. It is the answer to virtually all of our problems. And not taking control of this inner force, and instead, letting fear, pain, and repressed feelings run amok within us (rather than looking within and facing them), is the cause of all our problems, since by living in such a state, we will telementationally create such a world for ourselves since that is what our innermostness feels and believes.

Telementation is the key to our feeling deep satisfaction and happiness in life. But few know that telementation even exists; and fewer yet know how to exercise and control this power.

In this book I do include a tiny fraction of the science and philosophy involved telementation (especially in the next section), but mostly I discuss the specific technique for developing telementational abilities in daily life. *Telementation is a meditational pursuit, and a religious/spiritual way of life.* It is, therefore, *not* something you rush through for five minutes each day, or in a careless (unsoulful) manner. Telementation involves practicing the *daily meditation practice* of telementation and noticing the staggering effects of it in your life, and it *does not* involve conceptual analysis and philosophy. So it is only appropriate that this book focuses mostly on technique and the art of telementation, rather than on philosophy or other superfluous issues not directly connected to telementational practice and success in your life.

When most people first hear about telementation after being raised their entire life to believe reality involves something opposite of telementation, they respond in such a way that they usually fall into one of two groups:

(1)   Those who *reject* the theory of telementation outright, because it is such a startling thesis and such a shocking model of reality (in their eyes that are preconditioned to believe otherwise). It is too much of a paradigm shift for them to accept, and instead they go on believing the other, false, view of reality (which is called "cause and effect").

(2)   Those who *accept* the theory of telementation, but fail in implementing its principles in daily life because they are not motivated enough, don't care

enough, don't have proper instruction, or get scared of the incredible power of telementation.

Those who fall into camp 1 will never learn the art of telementation, of course. Those in camp 2 also will not learn it either, because they do not see telementation already the ruler of their life, and by that very fact they telementationally create a reality for themselves where telementation is nonsensical in their eyes. They are like Luke Skywalker in *The Empire Strikes Back*, where when Luke Skywalker said to Yoda, "I don't believe it" after Yoda telekinetically (i.e., telementationally) removed Skywalker's spaceship from the swamp, and where Yoda responded: "*That* is why you fail!"

Quantum Physics and Telementation

If indeed there exists such a cosmic hologram,
then every piece of the universe contains
information concerning the makeup
of the entire cosmos.

—Richard Gerber, *Vibrational Medicine*

What is the evidence for the existence of telementation? Is the study of it scientific? The only real proof or evidence that "professional" (i.e., "established," academic, university) science has presented that I know of, currently, for the theory of telementation, is from interpretations of quantum physics, especially the so-called Copenhagen Interpretation. I am not terribly concerned with this issue of giving scientific evidence for the existence of telementation, but I imagine some of the readers will be, and for that reason I will say a few things.

I am not sure if telementation can be a scientific theory, unless we have a widespread revolution in cultural thought. Science involves what people can see and agree on. For example, we can all agree that the sky is blue and that quantum particles "flicker" (on a computer screen in a lab); we can point to these, talk about them, and do experiments to do with them. Such perceptual situations are needed to carry out scientific pursuits. But telementation is not such an endeavor, since it is based deep in consciousness. Consciousness is not something we can take and place on the table and all stand back and analyze, and if we cannot, it may be difficult to bring it into the scientific domain. So, telementation is primarily a philosophy and a meditative art, and we need not trouble ourselves with trying to prove to others that it is real. If, however, we were, as a culture, all doing and succeeding at carrying out telementational meditation, we would have observable results, since we'd all see it working in our lives, and we could all talk about results we've each had, and telementation would be somewhat scientific. But, as I stated, that would take a culture-wide revolution in thought, interest, knowledge, and behavior, since currently we are so far from such a cultural state, and since so many are so wound up in television, shopping, and "this-n-that" to notice something like our innate telementation we possess that is co-creating the cosmos with all other sentient beings.

But, it is interesting to note that many scientists are coming to conclusions in their research that support the thesis that telementation is perhaps a correct theory of reality. It is no secret that the great founders of quantum physics endorsed the idea that reality (particles of energy) are created by *observation*,[4] and thus by consciousness (more technically put, that wave-functions are collapsed by acts of observation—i.e., acts of consciousness). "No elementary [particle] phenomenon is a real phenomenon until it is an observed phenomenon," according to the eminent physicist, John Wheeler.[5] This is a key feature of the Copenhagen Interpretation of quantum physics, which is not a science itself, but is a set of ideas and theories that have grown up around trying to explain some of the scientific experiments that have been carried out in the area of quantum mechanics (the study of the smallest entities known to exist). What is interesting about this theory is that it involves the idea that at least one aspect of our consciousness (the act of our perceiving) is *creating reality*, which could be as aspect of telementation.

In fact, this sort of quantum mysticism is quite widespread among physicists. For example, in his book about quantum physics and consciousness, J. Satinover writes: "At the [quantum]... level, matter itself actually looks and behaves (in the words of one physicist) 'more like a thought than like the cogs of a machine'."[6] This is a little different from the Copenhagen Interpretation just discussed, but what it involves, as the Copenhagen Interpretation also involves, is the idea that the prime matter of the cosmos and our thoughts are of the same sort of stuff ("thought stuff") and thus can influence each other (since thought stuff can influence other thought stuff, as our own inner minds show). So it is interesting that physics involves the idea that when we probe nature to the smallest realms we find energy that apparently is interacting with and/or created by our conscious processes. Since all of physical reality is composed of these particles (thoughts), then reality is overall a giant set of thoughts, or perhaps in sum one grand thought-stream, and this is very much in line with telementation: reality is a product of consciousness.

Continuing with this theme introduced in the Satinover quote above, quantum physicists have also discovered that reality is apparently *not* composed of matter, but rather of *non-matter*—the same sort of stuff that the mind is made of.[7] Malkowski writes:

> So does the brain create the self, and could it simply be the size of the human brain that gives us our ability to think in ways far different from those of animals? If it were, dolphins would be a higher order of being than we are, and they are not. It is the mind and the workings of the central executive, not brain size, that distinguishes us as sapient beings—the functioning and organizing of which has engineered the building of civilization. In this

way, the nature of the self can be viewed as abstract, and is the human consciousness that involves thought, perception, emotion, will, memory, and imagination.[8]

According to longtime consciousness researcher and University of California professor of physiology Benjamin Libet, the unity of human consciousness poses difficulties with traditional approaches to the brain/mind problem. After a long and distinguished career in neuroscience, Libet concludes that neural networks within the brain offer little insight into how subjective experience occurs. According to Libet, "A knowledge of nerve cell structures and functions can never in itself explain or describe conscious subjective experience." There is nothing in the brain suggesting that subjective experience—the role of the observer—is actually occurring.[9]

The famous philosopher Descartes was deeply troubled by the idea that mind and the world were of such different natures, and thus it may *not* be possible that they can interact, according to him. But we now know that he was wrong, since mind and the world (particles) are *both* non-matter[10], and thus may be able to influence one another—this is the cosmic process of telementation.

So there are a few areas of science and philosophy that lead to the idea that mind and world (particles) are not only the same sort of stuff, but also that they interact in a *two-way* telekinetic relationship.

The further we penetrate into matter, the less matter we find, and the more of ourselves (thought, feeling) we find. It's as if when we look into the heart of matter all throughout the cosmos, we find our innermost, most intimate selves *everywhere*. Cosmos is a product of, and a type of, thought and feeling-consciousness.

Telementation is Telekinesis

When all the images of the soul are taken away
and the soul can see only the single One, then the
pure being of the soul finds passively resting in
itself the pure, form-free being of divine unity,
when the being of the soul can bear nothing else
than the pure unity of God.

—Meister Eckhart

Telementation is a kind of *telekinesis*: the ability to move and alter matter with your consciousness alone. Telekinesis is usually thought of as being something spectacular, such as something out of the film *Star Wars: The Empire Strikes Back*, where, for example, Yoda was seen commanding rocks and spaceships to float around in the air with his Yoda-mind-powers. That sort of telekinesis may exist for certain experts in parapsychology, but that is not the sort of telekinesis I discuss in this book.

Rather, I discuss a "softer," but more broad-reaching sort of telekinesis in this book—that is what telementation is. Rather than being able to move rocks and trees with your mind in the present moment, in this book you will learn to be able to control *events* in the future (often the very *very* near future). I don't think you will learn to make rocks float, but you will learn to create an increase in the number of digits of your bank account, for example.

Telementation is the Power of the Universe

The human body... is a product of an organizing
field which, in common with all other fields, is
within, and subject to, the greater organizing
fields of the Universe.

—Dr. Leonard J. Ravitz, *Electrodynamic Man*

Although telementation is not difficult to master, I
don't think that learning telementation (the law of
attraction) is quite as easy as other authors often tell us it
is. Some other authors very optimistically tell us that
learning it is *so simple* that it is almost odd if you can't just
pick it up in 5 minutes with great success. Yes,
telementation is simple, but I disagree with the idea that
we can learn this simple technique effortlessly and
quickly. In fact I think it takes a bit of practice to get it
right, and after you do, *then* it becomes very easy.

Telementation involves a feeling- and thought-
mode that is always flowing deep inside of us, but one
which most of us are not used to being aware of, paying
attention to, or controlling. In fact, I think most do not
even know about this innermost energy within them and

they will likely even have some initial difficulty in locating it (seeing it, feeling it) within themselves.

Getting in touch with this power—this *feeling-power*—deep within us takes practice, and it is something that needs to be treated with care, because when you learn to steer and control this power, you will see it manifest things in physical reality, and you will be in awe over the incredible power of this force within you. It's the creative force of reality, and that's nothing to take lightly.

For these reasons, telementation is something we all need to move into slowly; doing so is very safe (and enjoyable), and you need not worry. As you learn how to exercise your telementational powers as a result of reading this book, don't rush it! You have plenty of time to learn it. Why don't you give yourself a month to get it figured out. Telementation is immensely powerful, and not using it correctly can cause you problems. I actually destroyed my car when I was learning how to carry out telementation due to my inexperience, my overzealousness, and due to my lack of understanding of what to do with uncontrolled thoughts (see below). So just take your time and do it right. Give yourself a month to learn it, introducing yourself with telementation with light projects (for example, attempt to will into existence something you can initially believe with utmost faith—try, for example, to will into existence that your best friend will call and talk to you out-of-the-blue about rainforests, if that's something she/he is not normally inclined to do regularly).

Telementation is not a simple plaything, as stated. Rather, telementation is:

(1)   the ultimate power of the universe,

(2)   the answer to all of humanity's problems (for individuals, and for society overall),

(3)   dangerous if not executed initially, in the early, learning stages, with care, and

(4)   it is something that requires one to restructure their innermost consciousness in a few ways in order to execute it properly (how to do this will be discussed below).

I have learned from so many others about telementation, and I am forever grateful to them for sharing this gift with me, but this book is meant to go beyond my teachers. This is because I was not able to gain expertise in the art of telementation until I learned my own techniques for carrying it out, and that is the aforementioned *feeling-based* telementation, which you will learn about in this book.

Restructuring "Autopilot" Consciousness

Through the flower I talk to the Infinite,

which is only a silent force.

—Pam Montgomery, *Plant Spirit Healing*

The Law of Attraction (telementation) should really be called the *Law of Focused Feeling*, or the *Law of Focusing*. That is because telementation depends on what consciousness is doing (what it is *focusing on*), not on what the universe is doing (*being attracted*). "Attraction"—and I am not sure exactly what "attracting" *really* means here, in the deep mechanical and philosophical sense—has to do with the mind and the cosmos, not just the mind-state. This is interesting, and worth exploring in another book, but to understand and have success at the technique of telementation, we merely need to focus on our consciousnesses solely (and then watch the cosmos respond), rather than on philosophy. Thus, I like the word "telementation," rather than "law of attraction," to describe this cosmic principle, since "telementation" is a word that focuses more on consciousness and telekinetic consciousness. Having success with telementation must be understood as a mind alteration and/or exercise, if you want to learn it and succeed at it. And it is only secondarily that you will change (attract) the cosmos in order to create reality as you want it to be. When a conscious being participates in telementation, she/he must *focus, know,* and *feel*—those are the keys to successful telementation, as I will show below, and the reader cannot underestimate the importance of those three words. Focusing inside changes the world outside.

I learned telementation myself just by reading books on the subject, and getting the hang of it through trial and error. I had to really work at it, learning through mistakes, until I saw repeatable results due to my focusing. Not any old feeling and/or thought within you will manifest an event in reality. If that were the case, then if you simply think of a blue dragon right now, one will appear before your eyes sometime shortly. That of course does not happen, and thus only some feelings are tied into, and participating in, the cosmic force of telementation. The key to this book is to help you find which feeling-streams within you are telementational, and then to amplify and steer them in your consciousness while making them ever-present in your awareness.

I did not have success with telementation until I *reconstructed my spontaneous moment-to-moment mental life.* This is of monumental importance. You will not succeed unless you alter the very bedrock of many aspects of the "autopilot consciousness" streaming through you from moment-to-moment. Even just doing this slightly makes all the difference in the world regarding your success at telementation. This may sound as if it is a difficult endeavor, but it is all quit easy, even effortless, to do, as you will see after you read the next few sections of this book.

All readers of this book should know what "autopilot consciousness" is, since it is streaming through you from moment-to-moment, and since it probably makes up most of what you have (erroneously) known yourself to be. Seifer writes:

> Most of our actions are due to automatic responses to stimuli. Gurdjieff and Ouspensky write that we spend most, if not all, of our life in an automatic pilot existence, which they call "waking-sleep." The mechanical state is quite similar to the behavior of inorganic or organic chemical reactions in that no real "thought" is claimed to be involved. The human/machine simply moves in a prescribed stimulus-response path.[11]

Let me put the matters we are discussing here in another way. If I sit and meditate and focus on a specific target to be manifested in my telementational work (for example, let's say I wanted to will into existence that my wife will have a particularly good day today), and I have successful meditation, but then after the meditation is done, I return to my moment-to-moment "autopilot consciousness" streaming through me, but that "autopilot consciousness" involved, before my meditation session, some pessimistic thoughts, such as, "oh, she is too busy," and "she will just be stressed out," then my mind will inadvertently carry out telementation by manifesting that "stressed out" target instead, and my wife will certainly not have a very good day. See how that works? It's your innermost feelings and thoughts that manifest in reality, and you cannot transform or keep track of *all* your innermost thoughts and feelings all the time. So, what is needed to be done is for you to change the mood, the vibe, the spirit, overall, of your innermost consciousness. Doing that ensures that really any thought or feeling that emerges in that deep realm will be filled with optimism, joy, and spirituality, and thus you will telementationally create for yourself a life of prosperity, satisfaction, happiness, and religiosity.

We all have tendencies to focus on pessimistic assumptions, mistakenly taking these assumptions as facts, holding them in our moment-to-moment "autopilot consciousness," thus allowing them to infect our innermost consciousness. These are the products of our bitterness over suffering we have undergone in the past and our consequent tendency to feel sorry for ourselves or remain angry over that suffering. Also, these pessimistic tendencies are the products of growing up in the culture we do and the cause and effect framework that we have been inculcated with. Cause and effect is a false, unverifiable philosophy that makes us feel helpless, as if it is the outer world that is shaping our lives, and thus we have little control over things. This is the opposite of telementation, the true philosophy, and it has infected nearly all of us. It certainly inhibited my telementational work when I was learning telementation.

For reasons such as these, I did not have success at telementation until I restructured my "autopilot consciousness" streaming through me, getting it to consist of a flux that *involved the optimistic and focused contents of consciousness that I deliberately inputted into all aspects of my consciousness.* Again, this is all very easy to do, as you will see. To give you a hint, the way to do this is to have frequent successful meditation sessions, even only for two or five minutes or so, at various times throughout the day, where you focus on the targets in reality that you want to manifest. When I learned to do this, frequently, and with this specific and repeatable right feeling-state in me, my "autopilot consciousness" rather quickly transformed into the contents of the focused telementation meditation session. In other words, doing very focused, short but frequent meditation sessions in pockets of time throughout the day, radically changed my entire mind permanently: if my frequent focusing sessions continually involved much optimism about my life, then shortly after my moment-to-moment autopilot consciousness would start to be imbued with optimism also. The meditation sessions that I directed flooded my consciousness, and soon my consciousness was transformed into the content, optimism, and joy of the meditation sessions.

It's Consciousness that Creates Reality, Rather than Cause-and-Effect

The morning wind forever blows, the poem of creation is uninterrupted; but few are the ears that hear it. Olympus is but the outside of the earth everywhere.

—Henry David Thoreau, *Walden*

Much of this has to do with, to paraphrase Yoda, is by "unlearning what we have learned." We have all been indirectly taught in our schools and on television that telementation does not exist—it's not mentioned, so it's overlooked, and other, non-telementational and non-verifiable theories of reality get instilled in our minds as alternatives. And instead, we become firmly set in the philosophy of cause and effect: the reason my friend called me to talk about rainforests was not because my mind and hers telementationally co-created that situation, but rather because specific events built upon each other, generated each other, resulting in a "causal chain" of events, where the end result was that my friend called me to talk about rainforests.

Let me ask you a question: What does this causal chain *look like*? In trying to answer that, you are probably scrambling to try to explain this event and that event that followed one another; for example, your friend had a desire to call, and that prompted her to pick up the phone, and so on. But did you see her thoughts which prompted her to pick up the phone? Answer: no. You assumed they were there, and that they were instrumental in this "causal chain." But let's assume that did happen, for the sake of argument. How did the *thought-event* "touch" the *pick-up-the-phone-event*, where the one followed (caused) the other? Answer: you don't know. In fact, you have *no idea* how to even begin to answer that question, because you cannot see these two events in the way you can see a brick, and you also cannot see them interact, and so you don't have language or concepts or experience that allows you to describe any of this. So how do we know that any of this even exists? And, do you see how the assumptions are piling up? We could go on to point out the problems, but the point is that you don't see any of the causal interactions, any of the so-called "causal chain", and thus, none of it is verifiable. So how do we really even know it's there? Answer: we don't, and we just assumed it is there because we believed one event happened first (thought-event), and then a second event followed it (the pick-up-the-phone-event). It's all a bunch of imprecise, murky philosophy that can not be verified. If you really want to know if something is real, you need to be able to verify it with your experience. You will never do that with cause-and-effect philosophy.

If we follow the unverifiable cause-and-effect philosophy, we will never have a reason for why the chain exists, what set it in motion, or why it was steered along the course that it was. We did not see the chain with our eyes, with all the events supposedly "bumping" into each other, supposedly generating each other, so how do we know that it's that chain, specifically, that is responsible for bringing that specific moment into existence? Answer: we don't. To understand how events come into existence, we need a theory we can *verify*; that we can *see*. And the only process of event-generation you will ever see is telementation. In other words, if you want to really *see* one state-of-affairs generate another one, with real reasons for the existence of an event, and a perceptible *source* for the existence of events, you will only be able to with the process of telementation.

With telementation, you can create an event in the world with your mind, and if you never had the volition to make the choice to do that in the first place, that event in the world never would have happened. In other words, *the event in the world depends on your volition to create it,* and it would have not existed otherwise. The *reason* for that event's existence is your telementation. This is a process of event-generation that you can see/experience, unlike the despiritualized, lower-age philosophy of cause-and-effect. Telementational event-generation is verifiable to your experience, and this has the power to prove to you that you are the creator of your life, your world, and we humans can have anything we want. Those who have taught us the philosophy of cause-and-effect (which is really the philosophy of fatalism) have misled us, tried to shove a non-verifiable pseudo-science down our throat. It's amazing that, somewhere in our past, we lost the knowledge of our inalienable telementational power. As Manley P. Hall has pointed out in his wonderful essay, "Mysteries of the Astral Light", the American Indians knew this power, and their "rain dance" was a telementation exercise. They knew this magic of the cosmos and their power to change the cosmos with their minds. But we are less advanced in our modern world, since we have lost this power and have learned that it is "normal" to just be pushed around by fate. Fate, or fatalism (the unverifiable theory that matter, the world, can influence your consciousness, you are somewhat or fully helpless against it doing so, and your mind cannot telekinetically transform matter), is merely the ignorance of telementation, the opposite of telementation.

We see *patterns* of events in nature (my friend calls me on the phone [cause] and eventually our conversation turns to discussing rainforests [effect]) over and over. This leads us to *believe* that there are invisible (not-experienceable) *connections* of some sort *from* the cause *to* the effect, as if the cause is responsible for bringing the effect into existence, rather than something else bringing it into existence. This unverifiable, pseudo scientific "connection theory" changes everything about our reality, and often to disagree with it, and scientists and psychologists will call people "mentally ill" for doing so. "Connection theory" leads us into thinking that if the economy collapses, well then it's the fault of the government, rather than our fear we put into the air telementationally. Certainly it is the fault of the government on one level, but on a vaster level, we are masters over ourselves telementationally, so if hardship comes our way, we ultimately caused it ourselves, and can quickly change it ourselves, too.

We don't *see* these eerie connections in "connection theory", so why are we "mentally ill" for not endorsing the existence of such invisible goblins? The point is this: we have been taught to conclude (assume) that cause-and-effect rules the world, but we have never really examined the evidence for that idea. Endorsing a cause-and-effect philosophy will be harmful to your telementational practice, since it is a fatalistic philosophy: if you believe events generate each other (rather than your free-will generating events), you may feel that you are not the architect of things, and you may feel that there is only so much you can to do change things. This fatalism can dwell in your moment-to-moment autopilot consciousness, thus negatively influencing your telementation work. But we all have belief in the cause-and-effect philosophy, whether we know it or not, so we must unlearn what we have learned.

For telementation to work for us (especially as we first learn it), we need to believe things happen *because our minds generate them*, not because other events generate them in causal chains of events ("cause and effect"). Cause-and-effect involves the idea that *things happen to you*, rather than the idea that *you happen to things* (the telementational idea). If we hold tight to the assumption that cause-and-effect are what solely control events, it will influence your "autopilot consciousness" streaming through you from moment-to-moment. You will think, believe, and feel that you are not the architect of your reality via telementation, but rather, to some degree, that *other events are the architects of your reality*. By holding those thoughts and feelings, you will telementationally create a situation where you are not in control of your reality, and you fail at telementation.

You Happen to Things

(Things Don't Happen To You)

Every phenomenon is like a dream, an illusion, a
bubble, a shadow; it is like dew and also like
lightening. So is all to be seen.

— *The Diamond Sutra*

So many things we have been taught in our culture
are detrimental to our having success at telementation, and
to our having the deep inner peace that telementation
involves. Ideas that we have ingrained in us like "the rich
get richer and the poor get poorer," "the young people of
the nation are not making good choices," "war is
inevitable," "it's a dog eat dog world," have been set into
our minds, and they manifest in reality precisely for that
reason: we are telementationally creating them by our
continuing to hold on to these beliefs.

The key to telementation is to believe and feel
fully, down to the core of your being, that *you happen to
things* (rather than that things happen to you), and that the
things you want to happen *will* happen. You need to
understand this to the point that that these sorts of beliefs
(or, more specifically, these sorts of *knowings*) become

part of your "autopilot consciousness" streaming through you from moment to moment, flowing effortlessly, spontaneously within you at all times, offsetting the implanted thoughts from culture.

This will all become easier and easier after you see telementation work a few times. It took me a long time to *really* understand that causation is not a correct philosophy of reality, and that, rather, telementation—*I happen to things*—describes what is actually going on in the world. But after I saw telementation really work just one time, my faith, and therefore my success, in the non-fatalistic telementational philosophy increased a thousand fold.

When I discovered telementation, my life completely changed right afterward. I soon figured out that *now* is a time of incredible hope and joy for humanity, because with telementation, as the book *The Secret* put it, we are on the verge of "the next human revolution", if we get the word out and show humanity how to take part in the transcendental magic of telementation.

Technique: *Knowing* the Target

Jesus replied, "I tell you the truth, if you have
faith and do not doubt, not only can you do what
was done to the fig tree, but also you can say to
this mountain, 'Go, throw yourself into the sea,'
and it will be done. If you believe, you will
receive whatever you ask for in prayer."

—Matthew 21:21-22

(New International Version)

Now I want to switch gears, to focus on the technique involved in carrying out telementation rather than on the philosophical background.

Above I said that the key to telementation is getting your deepest consciousness and feelings to *know*, *feel*, and *focus* on the targets (on what it is *you want*, those things are called "targets"). We now need to explore what these words mean in the context of successful telementational work. Keep in mind as you learn these meanings that the key to understanding these words is *simplicity*: there is nothing complicated about what these words mean.

- <u>Knowing</u> is merely having *total belief, convincing yourself completely,* down to the core of your being, that some target of your choice is real ("I believe and *know* without question that my wife will have a particularly good day today; I believe it so much that I *know* it is true!")

• <u>Feeling</u> just means that you know the realness of, the existence of, the target so assuredly deep within you that you *feel it* "in your bones", in the deepest recesses of your feelings in your spirit, in your innermost self

• <u>Focusing</u> merely means you are reprogramming your autopilot moment-to-moment consciousness, as discussed above

A person is always carrying out telementation in their life, whether they know if or not. In other words, a person's innermost consciousness and feeling-states are continually creating the reality of the world (with other conscious and telementational beings), whether they know if or not. But most people do not know that this is going on. Typically people never stop to look at their innermost feelings and thoughts to compare them to the events of the world to notice the one-to-one correspondence between them. Therefore, they are not making use of this ultimate power in the universe that they have flowing within them. And if they fear something bad will happen to them when they are dwelling in their autopilot consciousness, they will telementationally create its existence, or some approximation of its existence, simply because they are not in control of their special power. As Yoda said to Luke Skywalker during Luke's spiritual training: "Control! Control! You *must* learn control!" This is why *fear* is the ultimate destructive force for humanity.

The key to telementational meditation is to *control* (steer, shape, collaborate with, play with) your innermost consciousness so as to have a world you most desire materialize from your innermost consciousness, rather than the world you fear materialize from it. The telementational process is frequently undermined, because in your ordinary life, when you are going about your activities, your (mostly) subconscious (deep, innermost) thoughts and feelings hold doubts and pessimism about your life, mainly due to how you have been trained in your upbringing to believe *that* (bad) *things happen to me*, rather than *me happening to things* (or me having good happenings to things). These feelings and thoughts might be of the form of, "oh, x will never happen to me," "I will never get x," "I don't deserve x," I *hope* I get x" (hope is not *knowing*, not *focusing*, on a desired target, as I will discuss below), etc., and they all inundate your consciousness to disrupt productive telementational work.

Convincing Yourself

(At the Deepest Level)

Books about meditation have very little value for
one unless they become actively involved in the
practice. In learning about anything in life, there
is no adequate substitute for actually
doing the work.

—Les Kaye, *Zen at Work*

A student of mine once said that "telemention is
convincing yourself that such and such is true, wherein
you have no doubt it *will* be…"

There may be times you may think you really
believe something, but your deepest, often-hard-to-see,
somewhat hidden (to the natural/surface mind) feelings are
believing (knowing) *something else*, as I discussed above.
So, the art of telemention is to get oneself over that
point, to tip oneself across the edge, *from* any lingering or
subconscious disbelief about a given target, *to*
unquestioning and confident *knowing*, at the deepest
feeling-based level of your being.

This ultra-deep *knowing* consists of beliefs you are so convinced of *that you just know them to be true in your deepest feelings.* These must be held and made a continuous and regular part of one's innermost consciousness. Then you can control your innermost feelings and thoughts, and consequently shape your life. Holding these beliefs and knowings in your innermostness is not an act of strain or effort. Rather, what you do is merely restructure your innermostness by a few simple Buddhist meditative processes that I describe below. By restructuring, you automatically reshape your innermost mind and continuously telementationally create an ideal, healthy, and fulfilled reality for yourself (and for others, too).

Once you get the hang of it, you will start to believe there are no limits to your innermost power. I have been able to do astounding things such as alter weather and eliminate disease. This is all done by understanding and utilizing the real force of materiality: not the force of gravity or the force of magnetism, for example, but rather, the *force of your innermostness.* If you learn to do this, then you will become a master of telementation. If you do not do this, you will never succeed, and you will feel like your life consists of you being almost helplessly pushed around by the forces of physics (that's call fatalism). It's all or nothing.

Ethical Issues

In the end all frequencies and all expressions of
life are the same energy. We are each other.

—David Icke, *Children of the Matrix*

...consciousness itself is a kind of energy that is
integrally related to the cellular expression of the
physical body. As such, consciousness
participates in the continuous creation of either
health or illness.

—Richard Gerber, *Vibrational Medicine*[12]

One last thing before we get into some of the larger
issues in the next section. When your telementation
involves other people, you have an ethical obligation to
telementationally create situations that only bring them
happiness. I have never tried it, but I am guessing that
telementation could be used to harm others, if one so
desired such a situation. As stated, you cannot do this. You
might wonder: Well what's to stop someone from doing
that? Here's the answer.

The social world is ruled by the golden rule: the way you treat others is how they will treat you, and the better reality is for others, the better it is for you. Think about it: if your neighbor is poor, full of disease, illiterate, and pushed to criminality, do you think you want to live next to that person? Probably not; it would cause *you* trouble if they were impoverished in such a way. So it is in your interest for your neighbors to be healthy, wealthy, happy, and intelligent, for if they are, it will help you out. In this way, we can understand that the better condition humanity is in, the better it is for *you*. If you create pain and misery for another person, you are creating a world with more pain and misery than it had before. And since we all live together in the world, and since we all depend on and interact with one another, if there is misery in the pool of people it will affect us in ways that can only be negative. So there is no reason for you to do this since you will only contribute to creating a less optimal situation for yourself.

Also, there is no need to get things you need via hurting others. Since telementation exists and we can have seemingly anything we want once we merely master the technique of telementation, then we can get what we want merely with telementation, not via hurting somebody. So it makes no sense to hurt another with telementation. Doing so merely means one not only does not understand the process of telementation, *but one also is not deep in the spiritualization, joy, and consequent love for others that one undergoes* (described in the next few sections) *when one is successfully steeped in telementation.* For that reason, I don't think telementation is used to hurt others by those few people who understand the meditational process of it. If you are hurting others, it means you don't have the experience in telementation, and thus to have that experience you can't hurt others.

Getting Started:

Setting Up Daily Meditation Sessions

"You are entering a dramatic and exciting time.
There is a wave of energy passing through your
galaxy that is altering the course of all life it
touches. This wave affects the very nature of
energy and matter, bringing all matter into a
higher vibration. Although it is just beginning to
come to the earth plane, you may already be
feeling the effects of this higher vibration of
light. You may be receiving more insights,
having more frequent psychic and telepathic
experiences, and feeling a deeper need to know
your life purpose and put it into action. You
may feel you have less time and more to do, for
this wave changes the nature of time."

—Sanaya Roman, *Being Your Higher Self*, p.1

Now we really start to get to the meaty and
important issues. The next dozen sections are quite critical
to learning the art of telementation.

In the previous sections, I discussed how we find a
specific sort of control over, and the continuous alteration
of, our deep inner minds. But how is that accomplished?
Well, it's actually very straightforward and simple; you
just have to learn the basics of a few specific exercises and

then make the effort to carry them out somewhat frequently, and a change in your consciousness will follow.

The process is sort of like a hypothetical situation where you once believed that there were no UFOs, but then, let's say, you started seeing them over and over, and consequently you unquestionably believed there were UFOs after initially denying their existence because you had not seen any. Seeing is believing, and if your consciousness is inculcated with specific bits of repeated data/experience, it will impact, imbue, and alter your "autopilot" moment-to-moment consciousness. Having your mind exposed to a new belief over-and-over creates a situation where your mind takes on the new belief unquestionably, forgetting the old one. This is what we do in telementation: we use meditation and "focusing sessions" to reshape our inner minds, getting them filled-up with optimistic ideas about our lives and the world, supplanting our long-standing, pre-programmed negative ideas. Soon our innermostness radiates positiveness by being filled with the knowledge that we now have all the things (targets) we've dreamed of throughout our lives, but which we erroneously (fatalistically) thought we could never have.

Getting started with telementation involves little trial-runs to get the hang of telementation. We have to *see* telementation work, through little tests and exercises, involving easy tasks and goals, so that you can first see that the telementational power really works. This is very important, since initial basic successes build your faith in the telementation process. Building this faith is critical, since the more faith you have in telementation, the easier it is for you to deeply believe (know) that the targets of your practice are manifesting in reality.

It's easier to succeed at telementation, to deeply believe and know targets, if you believe and know that the whole process works. It's hard to convince yourself of targets if you are continually doubting what you are doing. Again, that's why initial simple test-runs in telementation are important to do when you are starting off, rather than jumping in and trying to get that big $50,000 check right away. Trying to run before you can crawl means you will likely just fall on your face. If you are trying to feel some target to believe in it and know it, it's much easier if you have seen targets materialize in the past. So, don't start off ambitious; start simple. You will have telementation mastered soon enough, and then you can go for the grandest targets of all, such as world peace. But get it right first so that you don't get frustrated and give up, as I have seen so many students do.

I will often say to myself a few times, "I *know* that x will happen tomorrow," or "I *know* that x happened today." For example, x might be my family has had a good day, or I will suddenly acquire $10,000, or something like that. Then I *feel*, very very deeply within myself, that these targets are real, that I have them *now*. This is carrying out meditation, and the key is the deep *feeling*. Deep inner feeling is the ultimate power of the cosmos; it can move mountains. I repeat this a number of times daily (as often as I can, in fact, but then again I really enjoy doing telementational meditation), and then what happens is that belief in the actuality of these targets *becomes* my deep inner consciousness, I really feel and believe (know) x to be real, and then, x is indeed manifested in the world.

If you really want a target to materialize, it is important to practice this introspective knowing and feeling frequently throughout a given day. You could, from time to time, get a target to materialize with just one little instance of feeling and knowing. But if you really want to have powerful, dependable results, over-and-over, you need to have, at various times throughout the day, relaxed, deep, enjoyable meditation sessions where you do nothing but feel yourself inside deeply, and then feel your chosen targets deeply. I have come to the habit of practicing this focusing almost constantly, at times at least, in holding certain feelings within my ever-flowing, deep-mind states. But then again, I really enjoy the practice of telementation, because it is so secure, powerful, and *holy* (see the next section).

The frequency of your feeling and knowing the targets throughout a given day is important because that's what builds the aforementioned continuous feeling in you; it's what leads to the greatly needed alteration of your innermostness. Altering your deep consciousness is quite straightforward, a three-step process:

1) You change the outlook of your life, focusing on the targets and happiness you want, by deliberately taking time to carry out the aforementioned meditations sessions.

2) With the periodic alteration of your consciousness with the meditation sessions mentioned in point 1, these sessions will be so powerful (when done right, with deep feeling, as discussed throughout this book), that they will overtake your weak and flimsy autopilot consciousness of your moment-to-moment life, and thus the mood, spirit, and feeling-energy of your meditation session will start to persist in you, beyond merely the times of your meditations sessions, and soon, your life will be flooded with the energy of your meditation sessions.

3) Upon doing what is mentioned in point 2, your deep inner consciousness will be affected by the power of your meditation sessions, and it will be reshaped.

If you try the meditations sessions, but you are having trouble achieving the all-important alteration in your deep psyche, then add a few more meditation sessions per day, or give it some more time to sink in and make the alteration to your psyche, or it is likely that you have not yet developed the deep feeling in the way discussed throughout this book.

Telementation Must be Enjoyable

or You Will Fail

Enlightenment is simply your natural state of *felt*
oneness with Being.

—Eckhart Tolle, *The Power of Now*

So how do you know if you've gotten to the deep
layer of feeling I am referring to in this book? Answer:
you will get to a point in your inward-looking
telementational meditation sessions where you will get
instances where you feel a contentment and joy that seems
to be coming from your act of looking inwardly at your
conscious feeling states. This experience may be very
brief, like a flash, or it could last hours or days, at varying
levels of intensity. When something like this is occurring,
*you know you are where you need to be in order to feel
your telementational targets into existence.* You can do
telementation at less intense of a state than this, but it is
likely a fluke if you have success over-and-over. Genuine,
disciplined telementation work that you can do over-and-
over at will, with reliable results, requires you take the
time to develop your deep, satisfied, joyous inner self. By
just merely practicing the focusing on feeling and ecstasy

at some deep level, the telementation will arise naturally. Deep meditation is powerful and deeply ecstatic—it is the essence of religious experience, the most powerful force in the universe.

I recommend that before you do anything in your telementational work, you learn to generate these little bits of quiet ecstasy within you, by merely relaxedly, unaggressively looking inward at your feeling-psyche. Get started on this first, and then after you get the hang of this for a few days or a week, implant telementation: tack-on targets to this feeling. First religious joy, then targets. I know you probably want to go right to the targets, being so excited for them to manifest; but trust me, you have time, a few days or a week, to learn the process. To have success, you must get in touch with your deep spiritual innermostness first. Learning to do that, in that order, now, will make all the difference to your transforming your life. Without your innermostness, that orb of ecstasy, you cannot do telementation. So, in your excitement for the manifestation of targets, don't forget that the targets are dependent on your innermost ecstatic self. The targets are just secondary, a product and flowering of the electrical-joy of your innate holiness that you and everyone else is made of.

If you are feeling your telementational work is laborious or unenjoyable, something you have to get your self to do (like fumigating the garage or cleaning the cat litter box), then you are definitely doing it wrong. This most likely means you are not operating on the level of religious experience, as just described. Also, it probably means you are focusing more on targets than on feeling—the inverse of what you should be doing. It is feeling (and religious experience) that drives telementation. So developing the deep religious feeling is so important; it's your place, your workspace you work from in your telementational life. The focusing on your innermostness is supposed to be utterly spiritual and joyful. You are hiding away in your own inner sanctum of your self, of infinite power and holiness. The legendary Japanese Zen philosopher, D.T. Suzuki, wrote,

> The great truth of Zen is possessed by everybody. Look into your own being and seek it not through others. Your own mind is above all forms... Zen has nothing to do with letters, words, or sutras. It only requests you to grasp the point directly and therein to find your peaceful abode.[1]

What you are, at your core, is holiness. Even the Bible says that in the first few lines: you are in God's

---

[1] Suzuki, D.T., 1964, *An Introduction to Zen Buddhism*, New York: Grove, p. 46.

image. In other words, you are *like God*, a holy light. This is also the primary tenet of Hinduism and Buddhism: if you look within, at the deepest point within you, you will see an infinite holy sunlight. So, to focus your attention there can only be a joy so great that it's like nothing you've felt before—even if you just scratch the surface of this level of *you* deep inside. It may take you some time for you to get in touch with this blissful, religious energy that you are; take your time. It's better to just properly learn to feel and identify it within you (or even just the "surface" of it within in you), past the egotistical shells, if you want future telementational success. And you may even have some initial success in telementation before you get to that point, but the ultimate goal of telementation is this sort of deep religiosity and happiness.

If you are having trouble focusing (seeing this happiness in your inner feeling states), you can do certain things to get yourself more focused. For example, you can eat gobs of extremely high-quality, organic, sugar-free and soy-free chocolate. This is an herb, and an extremely healthy one, and if you eat three bars or so, you will experience a specific sort of euphoria which is *incredibly and extremely* conducive to productive telementational focusing. Also, specific teas produce an extremely healthy herbal and religious high, such as damiana tea, which is a mild psychedelic. I have found that telementational consciousness just flows freely as Niagara Falls when I have this tea (but it requires *much* focus and discipline, so I only recommend this tea to you when you are somewhat experienced with telementation). Also, some music can also make one high and euphoric. Playing music that has beauty that entrances you, no matter what kind of music it is, is *enormously* productive for telementational practice. You have to experiment with what works for you. But do not underestimate the power of aides such as these. Find out which ones work for you and use them copiously if your telementational success requires it.

I also recommend that you eat healthy plant foods, high-quality oils (safflower, olive, hemp, and flax oils), indulge in vitamin-rich foods and herbs, avoid any non-natural foods as much as you can (non-natural means that it's not something right out of the ground, right out of the garden), and get adequate sleep. It is important to eat well and have adequate energy for the telementational work. These will help you in your practice, but you can have incredible success even if you are a fast-food junkie, though it may take you longer.

Your meditation sessions don't have to be contrived. You don't need incense and candles and Buddhist sitting postures. All you need is a quite moment to yourself, when you are falling asleep at night, checking the mailbox, walking up the stairs, using the bathroom, walking to your car, or on hold during a phone call. Those sorts of situations are perfect telementational meditation sessions. When you get experienced with telementation, you may even be able to do it in the noisy moments of life, too.

It may take you a few days or weeks to learn to instantly shift your attention to these meditation sessions (to instantly glance into your deep feeling state) during the busyness of your days, and when seconds earlier your mind was preoccupied with something else. But learning to make that shift, to get right into your meditative mode, right on the spot, is very important, especially if you can have a busy lifestyle. Until you can carry out these meditative moments at will, instantly, and productively, while you are looking for your car keys for example, I recommend that you make a point to find numerous quiet moments daily where you can just be alone, relax, enjoy the quite, and *focus*. Soon (maybe just a few days or weeks), after you become experienced in telementation, it will be as easy riding a bike—*no kidding*.

As mentioned above, there are some things that could happen to you in addition to telementational success when you learn to productively carry out these meditation sessions. What you are doing is *feeling yourself* in these sessions (this is the subject of the next section). You are taking your eyes and looking at yourself (to put it as Zen master Suzuki Roshi once did), taking your eyes you use to look at the world and using them to look at and feel your deepest feelings. Doing this is essential to telementational work, but also, it is the essence of Zen Buddhist meditation. So, if you carry out this practice enough, you may not only have telementational success, but you may also experience some level of deep Buddhistic bliss. If you get to this point, or even at the edges of this point, you will become positively addicted to your telementational work, because it will give you a joy, a freedom, and a loving-kindness that is so deep and wonderful, that you will want it all the time, and you will make efforts to stay in your telementational meditative mode as much as possible. Telementation at that level also will be quite effortless to you.

Zen Buddhism: The Art of Feeling Deeply

The most powerful force is Life-force.

—Trevor James Constable

Feeling deeply is the key to telementational success, so I will discuss it in a bit more detail in this section. To do that, let's discuss the all-important Zen Buddhism meditation a bit more. I cannot underestimate the importance of Zen Buddhism. I often sit back and ponder how I think it's just what the citizens of the world all really need in order to attain the power, satisfaction, and religiosity that they don't have (more specifically, that they have, but which they don't realize that they have since their egotistical consciousness conceals it). I was a Buddhist years and years before I assiduously started telementation meditation, and my background in Buddhism helped me immensely in my telementational pursuits. I am not suggesting that you need to become an expert in Zen meditation for telementation to work; I am merely stating that it can help you with telementation immensely if you want to make use of Zen Buddhism. If you are a Christian, you need not worry about your beliefs being compromised. Zen and Christianity have no conflicts between one another whatsoever. You can be a

Christian and be influenced by Buddhism and the only thing you will experience is an enhancement of your Christianity.

Ok, so let's get to the point. Here is the issue:

When you feel deeply, as discussed in the previous sections, what you are really doing is looking into yourself, looking at your deepest feelings, or, in other words, feeling your deepest feelings (you are feeling your feeling: feeling yourself). We really need to know how to do this in order to be able to control (shape, steer, play with) our innermost feeling domains, and the best way to learn this feeling of your deepest feelings is to learn a little bit about Zen meditation.

This section mainly discusses how you are to go about looking into your innermostness in order to feel yourself so you know you are feeling at the *deepest* level (which is the telementational level), rather than some surfacey, egotistical level above the deepest level.

Let's first get some background on the nature of our consciousnesses, and thus about ourselves, so we know what to look for when we look at our feelings: when we feel our feelings.

I have been truly surprised at how often students of mine report to me, after I tell them to look inside themselves and feel themselves as deeply as they can, *that they don't see anything "in there,"* or they don't know what they are supposed to be looking for. For that reason, I include this more technical section for those who have not thought about the differences between their outer self and their innerness. (Really, there is only the inner self, as you will see shortly.)

If you go into a closet, sit quietly, look at your consciousness, and try to find your *self,* you don't find anything that resembles a self, you only find things like feelings, thoughts, visualizations, and a few other sorts of items. But perhaps you notice something else interesting about the situation: what is it that's doing all this looking? This "entity," whatever it is, is called your *awareness.*

Awareness, or what is called *the mind's eye,* is a "piece" of your consciousness that is like an eye, a lens, for lack of better words, that *looks* at the other pieces of consciousness (whether they are inner-oriented [feelings, thoughts, etc.] or outer-oriented [images of the outer world] aspects of consciousness). The mind's eye can shift around, looking at different mental items. That's all that your surfacey, egotistical life has ever been: your mind's eye glancing around at other images and impressions in your consciousness, some of which you call *inner* (love, boredom, daydreaming thoughts about your upcoming vacation, etc.), and others of which you call *outer* (yellow, hard surface, matter, shape, sound, etc.). Really all the images and impressions in your consciousness are *inner*, since they are all experienced inside your consciousness (when you see a tree, you are actually looking at a mental-map [a "representation"] of a tree created in your sensorium; you believe what you are seeing is outside of you, at some distance away from you, but what you are seeing is really the inner impression/image in you, and thus it's an illusion that what you are seeing is outside of you: everything is *inner*), but let's move on and not get distracted with the metaphysics.

The *outer* **aspects of consciousness** are those experiences you have of things that you think are outside of, separated, and at-a-distance from your self and/or your body. So, when you see a frog in the morning sunlight, you may be inclined to think that you are "here", and the frog is "there", and thus the two of you are separate and distinct, since you are located in different places, and since you look differently and have different properties (green vs. fleshy color, hair versus no hair, etc.).

The *inner* **aspects of consciousness** are those experiences you have of things that you think are inside of you (in your consciousness), not separated from you, and not at a distance from you as a person. So, when you see a feeling come into your mind, you may be inclined to think that you and your thoughts and feelings are all located in one place, right where you are at, and thus all of these are not separate or distinct since they are located all in similar or the same places. Many Eastern philosophers think that these inner aspects of consciousness are the only items that exist; and Western philosophers have acknowledged for hundreds of years that these inner items are the only things we can prove exist. Even the awareness of the frog mentioned in the previous paragraph is, from your perspective, no more than a set of *internal images* (greenness, frog shape, etc.) that you (erroneously) believe to be outside of you.

In telementation we are concerned with the internal items, specifically feeling and thought—and more specifically, in telementational work we aim to generate specific ultra-deep feeling states in us and accompany them with certain beliefs and certain aspects of knowledge. What you are going to have to do is learn to "go" into your deepest feeling states whenever you like (this is hardest to master at first, and becomes easier and easier because it is so enjoyable), and then while in that mode you have to learn to hold certain thoughts and beliefs about your targets. This feeling deeply is *mandatory*; without it you will not succeed at telementation.

Feeling deeply amounts to you feeling yourself: you feel your deepest feeling state, much in the same way you would feel your emotions if you were looking at your emotions. This is merely the process of *looking at* your inner feeling objects. Start by looking at your ordinary, "everyday" emotions—do you feel bored, anxious, angry, hungry, cold, etc. *Start out simple: don't try to get to your deepest inner-spiritual feeling states right away.* This is supposed to be an effortless, relaxing, unforced process, and only with practice, repeated looking inwardly, will you learn to do this properly and ecstatically.

So, the more you do this simple looking at your emotions, the deeper you will eventually go, and the more powerful your feelings will become. (As an aside, this presents an interesting metaphysical issue: the more you look within—the more you focus your awareness—the more powerful it gets, as if this focusing can bring power to things. What if you were to focus this power into your hands, for example? Would you elevate the energy in your hands, so that you could, for example, place your hands on things and profoundly alter the energy in what you touch?[13]) After you do this for some time, you will "reach" what I call "the feeling mass" in paragraphs below: an unchanging state of feeling that is deep within us, and more basic or fundamental to our other more surfacey feelings (love, hate, anger, etc.). When you get to this point, your telementation will have the potential to be very advanced and powerful. You don't need to get to this state, however, in order to have spectacular results in telementation. It's just that at this deep point, at this point of the feeling mass, your telementation can become its most effective, and furthermore, this shift in one's attention can lead to nirvanic or quasi-nirvanic states, if you practice these meditational glances (feeling your feeling) frequently enough.

For some reason, when we focus on our feelings in the way just described, they grow more intense and deep: they gain power. The mind's eye does this when we deliberately use the mind's eye to focus on aspects of consciousness (when we feel our feeling). This is key to telementation, because we want to cause certain feelings and feeling-streams within us to become more powerful than the moment-to-moment autopilot consciousness, and thus to enable them to overpower those moment-to-moment thoughts, and to have command in creating material reality.

Consciousness is composed of three layers: ego, feeling mass, and nirvana:

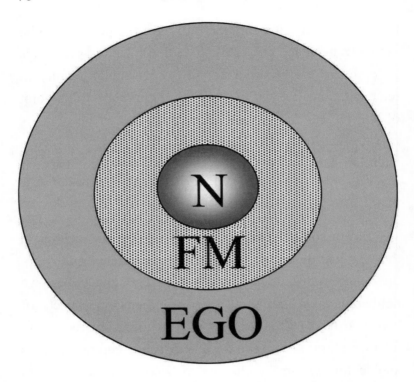

EGO (E) (outer shell): The ego is the consciousness of moment-to-moment autopilot life. It is largely composed of fear and desire, which streak through consciousness at a dizzying rate, even if the person is unaware of it (because she/he is not introspecting to see such). The ego covers the inner (true) nature of the person, and the ego can be considered to be not real, a false self, that is continually marked, according to Buddhists, by irrationality, despair, panic, and superficial happiness. The ego is the mask a person wears throughout her life.

Feeling Mass (FM): within a person, and under or behind the ego-shell, is a ever-present, seemingly unchanging, hum and vibration of intense feeling

Nirvana (N): at the core of the FM is found a domain of perfect peace and intelligence. This is the real you, your true being/self. In Hinduism, this aspect of the diagram is called Brahman and/or atman; in Buddhism it is called nirvana.

Incredibly successful telementational work is carried out at the feeling mass level. But it is important to know that you don't have to be there to have success in telementation. But I have seen telementation exhibit a law-like certainty and consistency when I am living and meditating at the feeling mass level. Telementation at the nirvanic level is instantaneous and utterly powerful, but it is not a topic I will explore in this book.

The Ego is *in motion*. In other words, its contents continually come and go (one minute I feel this way, the next I feel that way; now I am thinking about archery, and the next minute I am thinking about reading a book). But the inner dimensions (FM and N) are characterized by *stillness*. So, if an Eastern philosopher declares we are to "still the mind," she/he is actually declaring that we are to quiet, transcend (or maybe even destroy) the ego. FM and N are ineffable (they are not describable with language). Ego is merely a "copy machine," it reproduces the forms of outer-material reality in it: if you see a cat that you perceive is outside of you, you will reproduce an approximate thought-experience of this scene in your ego consciousness. Thus, your ego is merely a facsimile machine of what is believed to be outside of you. The ego is in this way a slave to what is (believed to be) outer. FM and N are not facsimile machines, in fact they are *freedom*, by definition.

The feeling mass is more-or-less a paranormal domain of relaxed intensity. It is intense feeling consciousness deep within all of our consciousnesses. Some philosophers assert that it is vital power that is in everything, and which is the ultimate power of the universe. To find the feeling mass (FM), merely start looking at your ordinary feelings within you, feel them deeply, and you will eventually start to see that at the heart of, or at the base of, all the ordinary feelings is an ever-present unchanging state of peace and solitude that involves high-energy feeling:

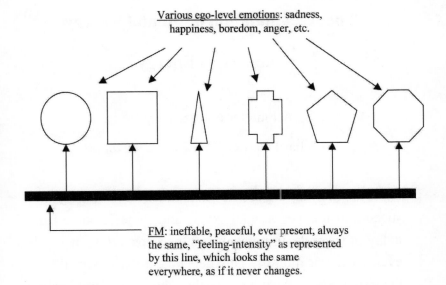

Various ego-level emotions: sadness, happiness, boredom, anger, etc.

FM: ineffable, peaceful, ever present, always the same, "feeling-intensity" as represented by this line, which looks the same everywhere, as if it never changes.

After some amount of time spent looking within these ordinary feeling you will start to notice an intense, unchanging feeling that is ever present, always the same in appearance, that is the feeling mass. Once you get used to looking at this state of peaceful feeling-intensity if you stare at this feeling mass, you can perform telementation at-will effortlessly, and joyously in this "place". (Also, you may eventually experience enormous religious states and religious happiness, as a result of this staring.)

The Accumulation of Mental Energy

and Astral Energy

All matter is frozen light!

—Richard Gerber, *Vibrational Medicine*

Often targets are not actualized immediately after successful telementational work, and there is some time-delay of seconds, minutes, hours, perhaps a day, or maybe even weeks or months. This depends, at least partially, on the productivity of your focusing, knowing, and feeling. But targets can be actualized immediately, also—powerful realization of targets can manifest just seconds after very productive telementational focusing was applied. The more focused your mind's eye is onto your deep feelings, the more you will build actual mental power deep within you, and the more of this vital force you build up, the more dramatic your telementational results will be.

There must be some sort of *accumulation* of mental energy (i.e., deep feeling states) required in order for any target to materialize. Mental energy builds when you focus your mind's eye on something. For example, if you look at a thought, or feel a feeling, your mind's eye is focusing on the thought or feeling, and they gain energy. *Where your focus (attention) goes, energy builds.* This is a facet of the tremendous mental power within you and *that is you*, but which modern science has virtually no understanding of, unfortunately. Your mind's eye, your concentration and your awareness, are some sort of an incredible power generator, where they *give energy to objects if the mind's eye/awareness is centered on them.* This is what many philosophers and shamans have referred to as magic, and it is a quality of what is often called the astral eye, or the astral body. This is perhaps the greatest unknown aspect of reality in the modern world, because it means that our greatest ability of our true self is unknown. People usually erroneously and tragically believe they are their ego. So, when we refer to a build-up of mental energy or astral energy, we are not referring to a build-up of energy of the ego-facade of consciousness, but rather of the deeper domains discussed above, such as the domain of the astral eye, the eye of the feeling mass.

The more successful the accumulation of mental energy, or what I am now calling *astral energy*, the more pronounced the target will materialize from the accumulated astral energy. We know that there must be such accumulation for focused telementation to occur, because if there were not, then any thought and feeling would be equal in telementational force to every other thought and feeling, and thus it would be the case that *every* passing thought or feeling would produce a materialization event. In other words, we all have spontaneous and uncontrolled thoughts, and if there was no mental accumulation needed to manifest telementational targets, then all of our thousands of random thoughts and feelings would constantly emerge. What if I had a flash of instantaneous thought of my computer blowing up in five seconds? If no significant accumulation of mental/astral energy was needed for this to materialize, then it would just be the case that my chance thought of my computer blowing up would lead to my computer indeed blowing up. But that does not happen. Whichever of my thoughts have the greatest power will manifest in reality.

This is one reason that we need not worry about our uncontrolled thoughts so much. (This seems to be a huge concern for people who are trying to learning the law of attraction, especially when they are in the beginning phase.) Often students have said to me that they are worried about uncontrolled thoughts materializing. But I always tell them that uncontrolled thoughts do not contain enough accumulation of mental energy to materialize in the world (unless they are giving them that energy), mainly due to the fact that other thoughts win-out in the telementation meditation process because they are the result of my focusing which intensifies them. Focusing our thoughts occurs when we look at them and feel them, when we couple them with our deep non-egotistical feeling. This builds more and more conscious energy the more we focus on them, and usually appropriate telementational work results in thoughts that have reasonable astral accumulation. Chance uncontrolled thoughts are nothing in comparison. The accumulation of astral energy is a real force, the ultimate force of the cosmos, and it comes from you.[14]

Your Inner Star-Seed

"Christ is all, and in all."

—Colossians 3:11 (King James Version)

After some time of practicing the techniques of the previous sections, you will get familiar with the different states within you. It is important to gain this familiarity. You will learn to identify the states within that produce telementation. You will learn to repeat the needed states for telementation, and put aside the unneeded ones. When you get to this point, you are ripe for extreme success, because whenever you want, you will be able to bring about telementation consciousness, as simple as it is to yawn or look up into the sky. This is perhaps the most important lesson in this book.

In my telementational practice, there is one specific, special *feeling of knowledge* that I get, and when I am there, I *know* beyond any shadow of a doubt that I will have telementational success, and I will manifest a desired target in material reality. I can get to this feeling over and over quickly, when I need to. I saw this early on in my telementational work: *there was this one specific intensive feeling and conscious state of knowledge that I would have deep within me, and when I had this feeling, this inner posture of confidence about a target, I would soon-after see the target of the telementation manifest in reality.* This is very important! All of you who want to learn telementation need to find the feeling stream and knowledge state within you that creates telementation. You need to find it, get familiar with it, remember it, learn just what it feels like, distinguish it from other feeling you have in you, practice locating it, learn to then steer it, and then learn to find and steer it quickly and readily. *This feeling state is the wellspring of reality and creation.*

This place within you is an amazing supernatural power source—almost something non-physical, holy, and/or extraterrestrial in its special religiosity. You have to learn to find, befriend, and steer it. You need to be able to quietly go to it whenever you want, relaxedly, but also quickly since you are so familiar with it. There are many streams of thought or feeling in you, but none like this wonderful, sacred place of worship. I call this place my *"inner star seed,"* because at its deepest, it turns the world into happiness and infinite light, like an infinite point of the sun.

You will notice that some targets are difficult to combine with that specific feeling, with your inner star seed, but other targets will combine with very easily. Sometimes it's the way you think about a target that needs to be changed. If you have doubt surrounding a target, and thus you can't get the proper telementational focusing, you may be able to change the target slightly wherein the doubt will vanish and the needed telementational feeling (your inner star seed) will arise.

For example, you may have a hard time getting your inner star seed to arise with the target "my wife will not have difficulty today at work," but you may effortlessly get your inner star seed to emerge with the target "my wife will have a wonderful day today." See, it's the same target, but approached differently in your mind. Sometimes you can visualize your target too; many try to do that also. But be careful with visualizing! I have seen ubiquitous failures with visualizing among my students, when they relied on visualizing in any way. In fact, I have never seen success with visualizing the target. *The point is the deep feeling*, the inner star seed! Nothing is more important than that in this book.

It may take you a few days or weeks to find your inner star seed and learn to get to it quickly. You first have to separate it out from other states within you, especially other imagination states. What you are looking for is raw feeling, vibrating, buzzing, deep within. It is different from the other streams of mentation within you. There are hypnogogic and hypnopompic streams. There are egotistical (ego) streams (ego stream are the streams that most people think are solely real). There are dream-state streams, psychic streams (these are associated with remote viewing, and they also hold tremendous power), and of course there are the telementational streams. You have to find these streams in you so you can do what you want with them.

Finding these streams is not a matter of getting serious, tensing up, and heading off like a hero to find them. Rather, it's just the opposite: you don't go anywhere, you don't tense up (you de-tense), and you are not serious. You just relax, de-tense yourself, let go of your probing and searching egoistical mind's endless worries, sit back, and watch what the mind contains and reveals. In that relaxed state, the different streams of consciousness will become apparent to you. Here's how the French philosopher Hubert Benoit describes Zen meditation:

> This effort of relaxation consists in a certain glance within. This inward glance, as we have said, is that which I make towards the centre of my whole being when I reply to the question: 'How are you feeling at this moment from every point of view at the same time?'[15]

> In practice, this work should entail inner gestures repeated, but short and light. It is not a question of

laboriously dwelling upon it as though there were there something to seize. There is nothing to seize. It is a question of voluntarily noting, as in the winking of an eye, instantaneous and perfectly simple, that I am conscious of myself globally in that second (through an effort to observe how I am conscious of myself in that second). I succeed instantaneously or not at all; if I do not succeed at all I will try again later (this may be a few seconds later, but the gesture should be carried out at one go. It is to my interest to make this gesture as often as possible, but which suppleness and discretion, disturbing as little as possible the course of my dualistic inner life...[16]

Here is more reasoning for why uncontrolled thoughts are not such a worry in telementational work: because, in my experience, the entire telementation process is at a mental plane often to a degree beyond the random, egotistical, everyday thought (which is the unfocussed, uncontrolled ever-changing discursive thought).

Frequency of Telementational

Meditation Sessions

Wind subsiding, the flowers still fall;
Bird crying, the mountain silence deepens.

—From the *Zenrin Kushu*

As mentioned, I have been puzzled by other authors I have read who have indicated that not only is the telementational work easy, but furthermore, it is something that need not be practiced often—just five minutes a day is "more than adequate," according to a CD currently out by one of the experts interviewed in the film, *The Secret*.[17]

That may work for some people, but for myself (and for every single student I have talked to involved in telementation work), I find that I must diligently (and happily) practice the telementational work, and I must diligently carry out the aforementioned restructuring and re-training of the deep subconscious feeling states, more than five minutes per day, in order to have success at telementation. Personally, I need to make significant portions of my day devoted to productive telementational-meditational exercises, generating the aforementioned deep feeling-states, for the desired targets to be actualized.

If I let up on my determination and regular practicing of the telementational practice, the targets come less and less, and eventually not at all. If there is a target that I really *really* want to materialize, I have to make sure to have at least ten or so minutes, two to five times a day, where I close everything out, go to a private or secret place, close the blinds, turn on appropriate music, or use brainwave or biofeedback devices, and where I deeply feel and *know* that the targets I am focusing on are real.

But, on the other hand, I have had times where, in passing, I merely just thought of something, as part of my daily mentation, but in a way where I was inadvertently carrying out light-level telementational work, and the target of my thinking was actualized shortly after. But this haphazard way of doing the telementational work is not what I believe is meant when I say that the telementational work is the most powerful force in the universe that you can tap into. To truly shape reality in a way that we wish it to be shaped, we must practice diligently in the way I have described above, gradually making it our way of life, which is a intensely spiritualized life: *peaceful intensity*, like a set of atoms quietly, fiercely, flashing in and out of existence, beyond the view of the egotistical human.

The First Law of Telementation:
You Won't Figure Out How Targets will
Manifest. Letting Go and Not Planning

We are living in a collective dream that we have
been manipulated to believe is sold and 'real'.

—David Icke, *Infinite Love is the Only Truth,*
Everything Else is Illusion

If you find yourself trying to figure out *how* the
telementational force will bring about the target of your
focus, you could damage the process with all the
conflicting thoughts (and the corresponding conflicting
feelings) you send in that process. Early in your practice,
some of this will be inevitable, and you will find yourself
doing this, especially after your first successes. Don't be
too hard on yourself for this error; who can help having
this curiosity. But it will pass quickly, because you will
soon see that when targets materialize, they never do in a
way that you would have anticipated. When you become
experienced in telementation, you will simply let go and
live, and you will feel the world around you, and you

won't worry about *how* the innermost-force will give you what you are telementationally willing. Mohr writes:

> If you focus on the target of having your bank account have one million dollars in it within six months, it is inevitable that you will start to imagine *how* that will happen. You will find yourself thinking, "Gee, I wonder if it will be the case if I will win the lottery; is that how I will get the million bucks?" It has been my experience that it is completely pointless, and even potentially distracting and harmful to the telementation process, to try to imagine how it will all work out, for the simple reasons that the telementational principle of the universe
>
> (1)   seems to always defy and go beyond our egotistical imaginations in many ways, such as in *how* the targets are realized (just when you think you can predict how a target will come about, it comes about in a completely surprising way that you never would've suspected), and
>
> (2)   seems to be almost infinitely creative in how it materializes targets.

In other words, it seems to be a quality of the telementational force that we cannot know how, by what process, it will bring about our targets.

I have spent time imagining *how* the telementational process will be carried out (especially early in my experience with telementation), and *never once* has it turned out that way. And, more interestingly, the target is very often realized in some entirely surprising, and *often miraculous* or totally unexpected way. When one sees this process occur, one loses the desire to wonder how the telementational process will be carried out, and instead, one just marvels mystified at the process itself after seeing it unfold.

It's almost as if the cosmic principle that is responsible for "listening" to our deepest thoughts and feelings, and thus creating reality out of them in then process of the telementational work, deliberately does not bring about our targets in the way we would guess they will come about. I have been endlessly amazed at how I would have never guessed that the targets that came about had done so as they did.

This is a first law of telementation.

The Second Law of Telementation:

Telementation Always Works

We are God's fellow workers; you are
God's field, God's building.

—1 Corinthians 3:9

In my earliest days of learning about telementation,
I would go out in my driveway and play basketball,
shooting with my eyes closed, or shooting backward shots,
where in both cases, I could not see the basketball hoop. I
found that when I got into a certain deep feeling state of
belief (my inner star seed), I would be able sink any shot
backwards or with my eyes closed. I remember one day
confidently and blissfully telling my students: "I don't
shoot the ball with my hands, I shoot it with my mind!
You do not need your eyes to play basketball. You do not
shoot the ball with your arms. You steer the ball with your
mind, driving it into the hoop with your consciousness." It
was from these early intellectual exercises that I deepened
my faith in telementation.

When I deeply feel and *know* that the future will be
x, because of productive telementational focusing, x
always manifests. When I am in my place where

telementation comes from—at my inner star seed—my steering that cosmic force of feeling within me always results in *powerful* telementation.

This is an interesting law of telementation: whatever your innermost consciousness feels is real about the world, *must become real* (unless the target is something impossible, like willing that a round square will pop into existence in the sky over West Lafayette, Indiana).

If, at the surface level of your mind, you think that the world is safe, but if deep within you, at deeper layers of your consciousness, you feel it is dangerous (but you may not know you are feeling these deep feelings, if you are not looking deeply within yourself, and re-training yourself deep within), and thus it may seem that telementation is not working. But that's only because you were not working at the deepest feeling-layers of your consciousness and soul.

Only working at those deepest layers is telementation successful, and at that level (the level of your inner star seed), it is always successful. This is a law of telementation: if you carry out focused consciousness from your inner star seed, your target will manifest. Just as water automatically freezes when conditions are right, telementation automatically occurs when conditions are in place.

This is a reason why many fail at telementation meditation: they do not work at the deep levels of consciousness, and they never even come close to grasping the religiously blissful inner star seed they possess.

They are not aware of this nexus, this fractal, between your force of innermostness and the cosmos. It is a linkage that is as tight as the relation between particles of the cosmos that are entangled: if we know what one is doing, we know precisely how the other will respond in a law-like manner, no exceptions.

Joy in Practicing

the Telementational Meditation

> When our internal environment is filled with war
> (conflict), that is what we align with in our
> external environment and, conversely, when our
> internal environment is filled with peace, we
> align with peace in our external environment
>
> —Pam Montgomery, *Plant Spirit Healing*

In previous sections I discussed how significant parts of my days are devoted to telementational practices. Some readers of this book may exclaim that that sounds like a lot of work, and not much fun. This may be true, but it is not for me, for two simple reasons:

(1)   I mix my practice with Buddhist mindfulness meditation,[18] which is inherently soothing and joyous, and

(2)   I shoot large and far with my telementational work, and thus when I am focusing (feeling, knowing) the target, I am for the most part bringing myself in a very joyful, spiritualized state, where I know that my future is wonderful, blissful, and thus there is much to live for.

Telementation offers the most positive and exciting outlook of any religious system or philosophy or way of life I know of.

If you are practicing meditation, telementational work, and taking care of yourself, the feelings needed for the telementational work will flow forth and sometimes truly explode and radiate from you so much that you may even get the feeling that others can see it bursting forth from you. It's a chain reaction and a feedback loop: the more you practice telementation, the more you get what you want in life, and the more you get what you want in life, the better you feel about life, and the better you feel, the better your telementational work will go.

Sometimes the telementational process results in immediate outcomes, other times it does not. Sometimes results are so amazing that it's as if money suddenly falls out of the sky—literally (if, that is, the target of the telementational focusing was to acquire money quickly). In the book and film *The Secret*, those interviewed talked about checks just suddenly arriving in their mailboxes. I thought that was silly when I heard that, but then it started happening to me during the times that money has been the target of my productive telementational work. I still am dumbfounded by that. You might think this violates the first law of telementation (you can't know how a target will come about), but I never knew how what checks would come, from who, for how much, and so on. It still shocks me.

Fear States

> Not to be able to stop thinking is a dreadful
> affliction, but we don't realize this because
> almost everybody is suffering from it, so it is
> considered normal. This incessant mental noise
> prevents you from finding that realm of inner
> stillness that is inseparable from Being. It also
> creates a false mind-made self that casts a shadow
> of fear and suffering.
>
> —Eckhart Tolle, *The Power of Now*

Often there is criticism of the law of attraction with the following objection: The victims of 9/11 or Darfur did not ask for their fate, nor did they telementationally cause it, so telementational is obviously ridiculous. But it is easy to see how this is a poor objection. We have already touched on this above: fear states materialize, and thus the more fear you have the more materialization, and a feedback loop starts that can quickly get out of control. This can happen with large groups of people. For example, in the weeks before the 9/11 attacks in New York in 2001, the mass media held many reports that there was great risk of an attack on the WTC complex. Could fear deep within the WTC complex workers have been the window that let the evildoers who carried out the attack move forward with it?

Take the case of Darfur, or something similar to it. Victims will have troops and bad characters initially coming into the streets. This sets up states of fear (which can be quite powerful, obviously). With that, the citizens will visualize and mentally dwell on fearful situations and the like in their consciousness more and more, and increasingly as the troops get more and more belligerent. This is a feedback loop:

Troop threat ➜ fear in citizens' minds ➜ visualization of fearful circumstances in citizens' minds ➜ visualization leads to *increased* troop threat (this is a materialization event) ➜ increased troop threat leads to *increased* fear in citizens' minds ➜ increased fear leads to increased visualization of fearful circumstances in the citizens' minds ➜ yet more troop terror ➜ and even more fear in citizens ➜ more visualization ➜ atrocities occur.

In summary, the more fear the citizens generate in their mental reality, the more the troops are empowered. After the second arrow, this entire feedback loop could have been cutoff, but the citizens in this situation did not know about telementation, and thus it cannot be cutoff. I am not saying that the victims of Darfur should have just sat down in the road, and meditated to shape their reality differently (though, this would have worked if they knew the telementational methods). It may have been beneficial for the victims of Darfur to have armed themselves, and prepared for the threat, because this preparation and self-preservation activity can bolster the inner consciousness that the victims were not helpless, and that leads to deep inner states, not of helplessness, but of power, and telementation would have burst forth (unbeknownst to them), thus shaping their reality differently. In other words, the victims would have lived in a state of believing that they were not in danger, and thus those beliefs would have brought forth the telementation needed to keep them safe. It is always good to live ones life as if the telementational targets are actualized, not as if they are far off and distant.

Uncontrolled Thoughts –

Of What Significance Are They?

Herbalists throughout time, and ours is no
exception, have remarked upon the fact that when
a person needs a plant, it is not uncommon for it
to begin growing nearby.

—Pam Montgomery, *Plant Spirit Healing*

Not all uncontrolled thoughts are negative. This is an area of significant concern among those interested in telementation. Usually when one has problems with uncontrolled thoughts, they are referring to fearful thoughts that pop into their mind, and usually this is merely a sign that the person in question has not excelled enough (i.e., practiced!) in telementation. But we cannot forget that we always have to be open, fresh, and ecstasy-centered in our telementational practice, not rigid, rote, or expert. As Zen master Shunryu Suzuki wrote, "in the expert's mind there are few options, in the beginner's mind there are many."

I have been a subscriber of email alerts from the makers of the film, *The Secret*. On October 29, 2007, I received the following interesting email:

A **Secret Scrolls** message from Rhonda Byrne, Creator of **The Secret**

"How do I stop my negative thoughts?" - is a question that I have been asked many times. If you have ever asked this question then you will feel such enormous relief in knowing the answer, because it is so simple. How do you stop negative thoughts? You plant *good* thoughts! When you try to stop negative thoughts, you are focusing on what you don't want - negative thoughts - and you will attract an abundance of them. They can never disappear if you are focused on them... It doesn't matter if you are trying to stop negative thoughts or control them or push them away, the result is the same. Your focus is on negative thoughts, and by the law of attraction you are inviting more of them to you.

The truth is always simple and it is always

stop negative thoughts, just plant *good* thoughts!

Deliberately plant good thoughts! You plant

good thoughts by making it a daily practice to

appreciate all the things in your day. Appreciate

your health, your car, your home, your <u>family,</u> your

job, your friends, your surroundings, your meals,

your pets, and the magnificent beauty of the day.

Compliment, praise, and give thanks to all things.

handwritten margin notes: GOD, Quartor, Be Kas, Tundra, Concours, Kayaks, Canoe, I AM

So don't give any attention to negative thoughts.
Don't worry about them. If any come, make light of
them, shrug them off, and let them be your
reminder to deliberately think more good thoughts
now...

Rhonda Byrne

In our daily lives, we all have flashes of thought
and feeling shooting through our consciousness at any
time. Much of this is often about practical matters, and to
do with how our minds prepare us for daily tasks, daily
social situations, and the basic issues of life. For example,
when you are in a conversation with a friend, your mind
will be role-playing to some degree, and you will be

thinking over how best to reply to comments the friend has made, what facial expressions to reveal, how best to say things, and so on. These are spontaneous and involuntary thoughts and feelings that continually permeate our minds at some level. This is a very complex and pervasive process, and it is going on inside of us all the time.

Much of these spontaneous and involuntary thoughts and feelings inevitably have to do with things you do not want to happen. For example, when you are walking up to a busy street with your young dog, you will have flashes of consciousness (thought and feeling) that involve something like this, "be careful, keep little Snuffy away from the cars." And your mind might go further (which you would notice if you were paying attention to what your thoughts were doing, as the deep process of telementation involves). This is all part of how the mind works, and such spontaneous and involuntary thoughts and feelings are normal, and they are there to keep you in a continual state of anticipating, predicting, and preparing for life in the external world all around you. This is the basic way we navigate through the world, and it is these involuntary and mostly subconscious thoughts that do not have the power to create materializations.

It may appear that these thoughts are giving mental attention to something undesirable: little Snuffy getting too close to the racing cars, or running out into the street. Does that mean that you will create the materialization of little Snuffy getting closer to the cars than you would let him? In other words, do these subconscious involuntary thoughts continually flashing about inside of us affect the materialization of reality that we create?

Well, I can tell you this: I have a truly continual stream of such experiences (why do you think I chose the example about the dog running into the street!?) and it has never been the case that these thoughts at this level of spontaneous, involuntary, uncontrolled, "auto-pilot" consciousness have materialized in the world. That is just not how the telementation-work manifests, and the thought and feeling levels at the level of the spontaneous and involuntary thoughts and feelings are apparently not the sort that generate materializations readily, and/or they are not strong enough to do so, unless they are sufficiently intense, which for the most part, they are not in our ordinary daily mentation (unlike the situation with the Darfur victims, as discussed in the previous section). We all have continual fears of things (death, robbery, economic problems, and the like) at some level, but they never affect so many of us throughout our lives, and thus this verifies that these involuntary inner processings do not materialize.

Being a rather strict Buddhist, I very often look at my own thoughts—something Buddhists make a living at doing. I find all sorts of spontaneous and involuntary thoughts shooting through my consciousness; some very scary, some fantastical, some very boring and routine. And I can tell you that the thoughts going on at this level of "auto-pilot consciousness"—at the level of the spontaneous and involuntary moment-to-moment thought—just don't get manifested in my life, except if they are very frequent or compulsive in nature. They are, therefore, not strong enough to give rise to materializations, due to the fact that the quality of these thoughts are as follows:

- There is less energy and focus in these thoughts. And telementational projects tend to expel and emanate much more of the force of innermostness. And Buddhistic states of consciousness (which, at some degree or other the telementational states are) are far more powerful than spontaneous moment-to-moment states, accumulating far more mental energy.

- Telementational work involves a deliberation and volition to put consciousness in a specific mode, and the spontaneous and involuntary moment-to-moment thought does not. This also leads to telementational work being more powerful in consciousness, as the previous bullet indicated. When you are focusing your mind's eye on feelings, they become empowered; it's as if your mind's eye is a power generator of incredible cosmic electricity. Your telementational work empowers target thoughts and feelings; spontaneous chance thoughts that are uncontrolled don't have this force

- As discussed above, not all mental operations have the same power in the telementational work. Fear is far less powerful than anticipation and the emotions associated with wishing. One moment of powerful, deep telementational work can generate an amazing result, while 100,000 spontaneous and involuntary moment-to-moment thoughts on a single

item   will   not   cause   anything   to   be
materialized

But what about when fears take over us, and
preoccupy our deep consciousness, thus inevitably and
inadvertently creating an undesired target? That is the
situation to be careful in—I have been there!—and that is
the only issue that makes telementation dangerous. But it
is easily remedied, if one merely knows what to do. This is
a real issue that is of concern, so I will discuss it at some
length.

I disagree with the writers of *The Secret* in saying
that the solution is to "control thoughts," if they mean by
this that we should try to push out some thoughts from our
mind, and only allow others.[19] This is because I don't
think they are wording the issue correctly. They are
discussing the issue as if we are to choose which thoughts
enter our minds and which do not, which is impossible.
Mohr writes:

That which you are secretly afraid of will come
first... Sit down quietly and do not think of a polar
bear for three minutes. You probably haven't ever
thought about polar bears as intensely as just then
in your entire life. Therefore: Everything that you

do not want and have as an image in your mind, at a minimum, blocks the true wish.[20]

I know from reading the book *The Secret* that what the authors actually mean is that a target of our telementation should be "not having uncontrolled thoughts." They are correct; I have tried that and it works incredibly well.

But still you might say, "What about situations where I have uncontrolled thoughts that I just don't want there? What do I do?" Here is the most important thing I can say about this issue:

It is best to just let these thoughts go, not to try to subdue or turn away from them, and not worry about them one bit. You will never be able to keep yourself from thinking these thoughts once they are set in motion in your mind, and if you do worry about them, turn away from them, try to subdue them, they will roar with ferocity.

So, what you need to do is when these thoughts and feelings come into view, you need to do two simple things:

(1)   immediately target the opposite of the feared situation (this is roughly what Rhonda Byrne was suggesting in the email above), using powerful telementational work to carry out this opposite-target. (This will be cumbersome at first, but you will quickly get used to it, and it will become routine, and soon you will be so unafraid of the uncontrolled and undesired thoughts that they will not even come to you. Again, this may be a quick process. I have had very little problems with uncontrolled thoughts during my years doing telementation, and most problems were at the very beginning stages of my learning about telementation.

(2)   You should target the following: I *know* that my thoughts will not be plagued or filled with undesirable and uncontrolled thoughts.

Setbacks

Come my friends,

'Tis not too late to seek a newer world,

For my purpose holds to sail beyond the sunset.

And though we are not now that strength which in old days moved earth and heaven,

That which we are, *we are!* One equal temper of heroic hearts.

Made weak by time and fate, but strong, in will, to strive, to seek, to find, and not to yield.

—Alfred Lord Tennyson

So your concentration and focus is good, and you are materializing many targets, but does the telementational work *always* yield success? The answer is no, but rarely is the answer no—and there are various reasons for it.

When telementational work is unsuccessful, there are several possible reasons:

(1)   The telementational work is still in process, and it has not been realized yet. You may be expecting a specific time that the telementation target is to be realized, but it is merely taking longer than you are

anticipating, and thus the telementation failure is not yet a failure.

(2)   Subconscious (unknown) doubt. You do not have adequate faith and focus in the target. You may believe you have adequate focus, but you do not, and there are significant subconscious doubtings occurring in your subjectivity.

(3)   There simply are times when telementational work won't actualize, such as when the target is something impossible, like focusing on seeing a seeing person without eyes, or seeing a round square. This point is often combined with point 2.

(4)   You are working against another consciousness or against other consciousnesses. For example, if you focus on world peace, but millions of other people are filled with wrath and savage anger, with blood-fury in their hearts over other people, you will be outnumbered dramatically, and thus your focus target will not be realized. This is very common when you are doing telementational work in a way where your target is another person's

behavior: "I believe my wife will be happy today," for example. But, if you excel enough at telementation, your conscious telementational efforts can overpower all other consciousnesses in the world, and you can bring about world peace, for example.

(5)   The telementational work is functioning in more of an approximate manner. You are expecting your target to be realized in just the right way, but it is being realized in a way that is only partially in the way you are focusing, or in steps, and thus you imagine that your target it fully not realized, which is not true. For example, if you focus on money falling into your lap as a target, and then you go out and get a loan, you might not understand that the loan was the realization (even if not quite what you were looking for).

Crisis Can Crush

Productive Telementational Work

"It is about the alive act of moment-by-moment
listening to the flashes of thought at the periphery
of perception, and responding..."

—Michele Cassou and Stewart Cubley,

Life, Paint, and Passion

Often people will have some preliminary success with the telementational work, thinking they've mastered it, only to have a crisis arise that then rattles the person completely, wherein fear, worry, and lack of focus takes over, dominates, and maybe even crushes the person. In this process, the telementational work becomes virtually nonexistent, even though there was some preliminary progress initially. Then, in this state of devastation, the person emanates dread, fear, defeatism, and anger—all of which become the objects of consciousness, and thus become the inadvertent products of telementational work. This is why people often have everything about their lives fall apart at once: when it rains it pours.

I have been in these sorts of crisis times—believe me! I was in a situation in late February 2009 where I was so panicked and afraid that I thought my life was ending. And I can tell you, I did grab my bearings and got the telementational work going. I do not think I would have been able to get it going if I was not already quite experienced in it, however, but it's hard to tell.

Also, the telementational work was nearly instantly successful, and my dire situation turned around immediately. Back at that time I was noting to myself how much the whole situation illustrated how fear states can get out of control, and can telementationally create dire circumstances for us—especially if we are not prepared and ready to attack the situation with our telementational meditation right away. But the important point is that even in this sort of a situation, where fear completely overcame me, those states were not strong enough to fully block out the greater force of telementation. All I had to do, in my panic, was take a moment, go sit in my bedroom and focus for about a minute or two, and thereafter I was in my telementational mode, in control of the situation, willing a good outcome to the situation. And wow was there a good outcome, I found, as the months after showed! The expert in telementation certainly knows what it means when they hear the expression that hard times lead to good.

The Telementational Way of Life

The other thing we must realize… is that what is
to happen [to us in our future] will be determined
by the thoughts and feelings of the people on the
planet. If we change our consciousness we can
change the way in which the whole drama
unfolds, regardless of any prophecy. We are
creating our reality. We are creating each new
collective reality every moment. Our thoughts
and feelings are far more powerful than we could
ever imagine. For the most part, we have thus far
taken little or no responsibility for them. That is
changing, changing so quickly that a whole new
possibility never before dreamed of is emerging.

—Bob Frissell, *Nothing in This Book Is True, But
It's Exactly How Things Are*[21]

When one becomes a bit experienced in
telementation (and this may only take a few days or
weeks), it is as of the positiveness of the practice, and the
focused targeting, floods one's consciousness, one's feeling
and being, leaving the person overjoyed, preoccupying

them at all moments, endlessly filling them with religious feeling, and filling those proximate to them with joy.

The key is to get to *automatized telementational work*. For example, each day I get up in the morning and have telementational sessions where a target might be, "today will be a wonderful day." Focus on this target, *know* this target, and by the law of the cosmos, that day therein must be wonderful.

It is critical to know that one can perform productive telementational meditation for deep inner peace and intelligence right amid any activity of life, once you get experienced enough in telementation.

With practice and effort, and drive to be a parapsychologically gifted person, you can attain this inner peace and telementation through the chaos of your daily life, such as even during a presentation, lecture, traffic jam, argument, and so on—times which many would imagine this work cannot be done. This comes with experience.

The subconscious mind is a repeating and looping program, which is far more powerful, complex, and critical to life. This subconscious program, and its basic structure, is created firmly by age seven.[22] This subconscious contains our deepest feelings, and thus comprises a thick and powerful instrument for telementational work. So, many of us have saddened and damaged subconsciousnesses, due to what happened to us and what people told us when we were young. The idea is to recreate and retrain the subconscious with telementational work, and this will allow for a new way of life spontaneously based on telementational work.

All of us have been beaten up through our lives. We all have deep pains and resentments, deep longings, and forlornness over dreams unfulfilled. Even if you are not aware of this on a daily basis, your subconscious is, and it lives from these let-downs. If you doubt this, then just close your eyes, find and feel your feelings, look at your feelings, and you will see what I mean. We all need to change this needless state of being; that is done with the aforementioned restructuring of deep inner consciousness. Recreating the subconsciousness and the self is difficult but essential work, if one would like to fully utilize the telementational force.

Works Cited

Atkinson, William Walker. 2007 (1912). *Mind Power: The Secret of Mental Magic*. Cosimo: New York.

Backster, Cleve. 2003. *Primary Perception: Biocommunication with Plants, Living Foods, and Human Cells*. White Rose Millennium Press: Anza, CA.

Behrend, Genevieve. 1980 (1951). *Your Invisible Power: The Mental Science of Thomas Troward*. Camarillo, CA: DeVorss Publications.

Benoit, Hubert. 1990 (1955). *Zen and the Psychology of Transformation*. Rochester VT: Inner Traditions International.

Blackmore, Susan. 2004. *Consciousness: An Introduction*. New York: Oxford University Press.

Cassou, Michele, and Cubley, Stewart. 1995. *Life, Paint, and Passion*. New York: Tarcher/Putnam.

d'arc, John. 2000, *Phenomenal World*. Escondido, CA: The Book Tree.

Frissell, Bob. 2002 (1994). *Nothing in this Book is True, But It's Exactly How Things Are*. Third Edition. Berkeley: Frog Ltd.

Gaunt, Bonnie. 2000. *Beginnings: The Sacred Design*. Adventures Unlimited Press.

Gerber, Richard. 1988. *Vibrational Medicine*. Santa Fe: Bear and Company.

Gordon, Richard. 2006 (1999). *Quantum Touch: The Power to Heal*. Berkeley, CA: North Atlantic Books.

Grupp, Jeffrey. 2006. "Mereological Nihilism: Quantum Atomism and the Impossibility of Material Constitution," *Axiomathes: An International Journal in Ontology and Cognitive Systems*, Vol. 16, No. 3, 2006, pp. 245-386.

Herbert, Nick. 1985. *Quantum Reality: Beyond the New Physics, an Excursion into Metaphysics*. New York: Anchor Books/Doubleday.

Icke, David. 2005. *Infinite Love is the Only Truth; Everything Else is Just Illusion. Exposing the Dreamworld We Believe to be 'Real'*. Wildwood, USA: Bridge of Love Publications USA.

Lipton, Bruce. 2005. *The Biology of Belief.* Mountain of Love/Elite Books.

Malkowski, Edward F. 2007. *The Spiritual Technology of Ancient Egypt.* Rochester, VT: Inner Traditions.

Mohr, Barbel. 2001. *The Conscious Ordering Service.* Charlottesville, VA: Hampton Roads Publishing Company.

Santinover, Jeffrey. 2001. *The Quantum Brain.* New York: Wiley.

Seifer, Marc. 2008. *Transcending the Speed of Light: Consciousness, Quantum Physics, and the Fifth Dimension.* Rochester, VT: Inner Traditions.

Skrbina, David. 2005. *Panpsychism in the West.* Cambridge: MIT Press.

Targ, Russell. 2004. *Limitless Mind.* New World Library.

Tiller, William. 1997. *Science and Human Transformation.* Pavior.

Notes

[1] Behrend 1980, 17.

[2] Actually, I have borrowed the word "telementation" from William Atkinson from his wonderful book, *Mind Power,* and I have changed the definition slightly, to make up for this lack of focus on feeling that others have inadvertently portrayed to be associated with the law of attraction.

[3] Rense Radio Show, www.rense.com, Oct. 1, 2007.

[4] Herbert 1985, 17.

[5] Quoted in Herbert 1985, 18.

[6] Satinover 2001, 7.

[7] See Grupp 2006. I write there that the mind is non-matter because if you were to open up my head and brain and look into me to find my mind, you would *not* find it, you would only find blood, fatty acids, brain cells, and the like, but never something like the phenomenological entities called "thought," "the feeling of love," or "the feeling of anger", for example. That is evidence that the mind is not the same order of material that the brain is, and that it might not be matter at all.

[8] Malkowski 2007, 58-59.

[9] Malkowski 2007, 70-71.

[10] See Grupp 2006.

[11] Seifer 2008, 19.

[12] Gerber 1988, 44.

[13] See Thompson 2006 for more information.

[14] See Richard Gordon's book, *Quantum-Touch* for more information on this issue.

[15] Benoit 1990, 85.

[16] Ibid., 131.

[17] For those of you who can figure out who I am referring to, I don't not mean to belittle this person in any way, since I personally feel they have been an excellent teacher for me, especially with this short CD that he put out. I merely disagree with him on this one issue of frequency.

[18] I believe that this is very beneficial to the telementational work. If the reader wants to learn how to carry out Buddhist mindfulness meditation, I recommend the book, *The Supreme Doctrine*, by Hubert Benoit, and the book *Life, Paint, and Passion*, by Cassou and Cubley. Buddhist mindfulness meditation is not a religious practice in the traditional sense, since it does not involve any beliefs or God or gods. Rather, it is a system of transformation of consciousness, from ordinary consciousness to the aforementioned deep feeling states (and further than that, if one pursues it).

[19] It may be the case that by "control thoughts" that they mean to telementationally crease a situation where uncontrolled thoughts do not enter your consciousness (i.e., telementationally making *the having of only desired thoughts* a target of our telementation), since they do bring that up in The Secret. But there are other times that they seem to suggest the other type of controlling of thoughts: trying to only allow some thoughts into consciousness, not others.

[20] Mohr 2001, 6.

[21] Frissell, 2002, 16.

[22] For more information on these issues, see Lipton 2005. Also see the Rense Radio Show (www.rense.com), the December 21, 2005 show, for a powerful interview with Lipton.

More Books by Prof. Jeffrey Grupp

LIGHT, UFOLOGY and ECSTASY
There is a divine dimension everywhere in the universe. It is the Creator of all moments in time and of all existence. It is both inside your consciousness (1 Cor. 3:9: "You are God's field, God's building"), and omnipresent in the universe. It is freedom, compassion, and an ineffable joy. All things seek to flow with it, mimic it. It is often called ecstasy, or light, divine, the transcendent, or God, and it is the basis of all our religions. Awareness of this God-ecstasy is the highest task in life.

In *Light, Ufology and Ecstasy*, Prof. Grupp explains spirituality and religion as vehicles of this ecstasy, the history of this technique of ecstasy, and the ultra-advanced ancient civilizations who brought it to us. Most of all, he describes how to carry out the meditation and prayer exercises simply but in detail, so that any reader can open up their inner God-communion. Release in 2011.

THE TELESCREEN
The Telescreen is the pervasive media screen put in front of, and injected into, the eyes and ears of humans in the American electronic techno-culture. This begins from birth, and creates consciousness throughout life. But the consciousness created is not a genuine human consciousness, but rather is a less-than-human despiritualized semi-consciousness. 2009, 199 pages, $14.95.

CORPORATISM: *the Secret Government of the New World Order.*
Corporations control all basic resources of the world, all the governments and institutions, and prevent us from solving humanity's problems. Their New World Order plan is the global "prison planet" that Hitler was aiming for. 2008, 408 pages, $16.95.

THE INVISIBLE GOVERNMENT
America is going into revolution. But even before it's fully underway, there is tremendous evidence that the New World Order is hijacking and steering the revolution — taking it away from the people, and turning it into a divide-and-conquer operation: where the highest echelon of the New World Order works for the annihilation and sacrifice of the lower echelon ("the puppets") by the people of the world. Such operations are routine in history (Hitler, Bolshevik revolution, etc.), and another one is already underway. Release in 2011.

More from Tree of Life Books

Acres of Diamonds. You, too, can find your fortune — if you know where to look. The inspirational classic. $10.95.

The Unknown Life of Jesus Christ. Where was Jesus and what did he do from age 12 to 30? Adventures of discovery: the ancient manuscript in a Tibetan lamasery. $9.95.

The Prophet of the Dead Sea Scrolls. Origins of the New Testament in the mysteries and devotions of the Essenes, Jesus' own sect. Eye-opening teachings still ahead of our time. $11.95.

Saving the Savior. All the evidence, old, new, charts, photos, that Jesus survived the Cross and went to teach in Kashmir. $19.95.

More from Progressive Press

Five by Webster Griffin Tarpley, Expert Critic of Oligarchy:
Surviving the Cataclysm: Your Guide through the Greatest Financial Crisis in Human History. Deregulation and derivatives were programmed to blow US economy. 920 pp, $25.00.

Barack H. Obama: The Unauthorized Biography. The definitive expose of a corrupt and pliable politico. Nov. 2008, 595 pp, $19.95.

Obama — The Postmodern Coup. The Trilateral Commission's dangerously deceptive puppet. 2008-2009, 320 pp, $15.95.

9/11 Synthetic Terror: Made in USA. The masterful account of state-sponsored false-flag terrorism. 2005, 512 pp, $17.95.

George Bush: the Unauthorized Biography. The many incredible chapters of a political crime dynasty. 1992, 700 pp, $19.95.

Three new books by F. Wm. Engdahl:
Seeds of Destruction. They're out to control the world by locking up the basis of our survival: patenting our crops. 340 pp, $24.95

Full Spectrum Dominance. Militarizing land, sea, air, space, outer space, cyberspace, media, movements, society. 268 pp., $23.95

Gods of Money. Wall Street and the Death of the American Century. The banksters stop at nothing: setting world wars, nuking cities, keeping our world in chaos and corruption. 398 pp., $24.95

DVDs

Four from Adam Curtis, maverick producer of BBC4. $7.95 each.

The Power of Nightmares. The government keeps the terror phantom going — keeping the government in power. 3 hrs.

The Century of Self. Freud, Bernays, and mass-market materialism: seducing the ego for power and profit. 4 hrs.

The Trap. The bane of materialistic behaviorism on society, health, education. A very intelligent film. 3 hrs.

The Living Dead. History is manipulated to control the now. 3 hrs.

www.treelifebooks.com ~ www.progressivepress.com